T

and

the Spirit

My Journey to Becoming a Christian Spiritualist

Thomas E. Williams

The Way and the Spirit

My Journey to Becoming a Christian Spiritualist

by Thomas E. Williams

Additional contributions by Justin T. Williams

Cover design by Justin T. Williams

Copyright 2018 by Thomas E. Williams.

All rights reserved.

Author may be contacted at wayandspirit@gmail.com.

Scripture quotations marked (NLT) are taken from the Holy Bible, New Living Translation, copyright ©1996, 2004, 2007, 2013, 2015 by Tyndale House Foundation. Used by permission of Tyndale House Publishers, Inc., Carol Stream, Illinois 60188. All rights reserved.

Disclaimer:

The information contained in this book was compiled from sources believed to be reliable. The information presented as being personal experiences of the author is true. Other information is based on various events including life experience, opinion, known facts, and generally accepted knowledge. The opinions expressed in this book unless otherwise stated should be considered to be the opinions of the author only and are not necessarily the opinion of any church, organization, or other individual. Names and titles may have been changed to protect individuals. Any resemblance to any real person living or dead should be overlooked and not taken seriously. This information is intended to be used for informational and/or entertainment purposes. It is not to be considered a gospel according to any known or unknown saint of any religion or culture of any kind anywhere. An ergonomically correct environment, sufficient lighting, and neutral posture are recommended while reading this book. This book should not be read while driving or operating machinery including, but not limited to, heavy machinery and Smart cars. Contents may settle during reading. No warranty is expressed or implied. Not responsible for direct, indirect, incidental or consequential damages resulting from any defect, error, or failure to perform. Void where prohibited. May be too intense for some readers. Freshest if consumed as soon as possible. Keep cool; process promptly. Subject to change without notice. All times referred to may be approximate rather than exact. Printing may, in time, fade and may disappear if erased. Pages may, in time, yellow and/or tear and eventually disintegrate. Keep away from fire or flame. Soggy when wet.

Post office will not deliver without postage. No animals were harmed in the writing of this book. Beware of dogs. Author is elderly. Author suffered a traumatic brain injury in 2011 which may or may not have lingering effects. Reproduction strictly prohibited without the expressed written consent of the author. Any trademark mentioned herein appears for purposes of identification only. No assembly required. Batteries not included and should, in most cases, not be needed. One size fits all.

Please note the majority of the quoted scriptures contained in this book are from the King James Version of *The Holy Bible*. This version is public domain and may be freely quoted. It is suggested that if this version of the Bible is confusing to the reader another version more easily understood be consulted.

Dedication

This book is dedicated to my children. Though for some people it is a spouse or a mentor who has kept them grounded and inspired, for me it has been my four children who came into my life over a period of nearly twenty-one years. I learned a lot from my children when they were young about how they perceived things through their eyes and in their minds. Their views at times caused me to re-evaluate my own. Sometimes profound realizations come through simple child-like observations. Now as adults, they still amaze me with their thoughts and observations.

I also dedicate this book to anyone who, like me, is seeking the truth of our spirituality and purpose on this planet.

Contents

Introduction i

Part One: Conflicts in Christianity 1

    Conflicting Christian Teachings 3

    Is *The Holy Bible* the Infallible Word of God? 13

    Organized Religion and Today's Christian Church 41

    Out With the Old and In With the New 61

Part Two: Seeking Truth in Spiritualism 75

    Message Received Loud and Clear 77

    Praying to Die 89

    What Changed My Beliefs? 93

    Should I Believe What Spiritualism Teaches? 101

    Questions and Beliefs 117

    Free Advice 145

Epilogue 153

Information About Spiritualism 157

About the Author 185

Introduction

All truths are easy to understand once they are discovered; the point is to discover them. — Galileo Galilei

My purpose in writing this book is not to explain Spiritualism and all it has to offer, but rather to provide somewhat of an introduction to Spiritualism and tell of how I came to learn of it and become interested in knowing more about it. It is my hope that by reading this book your interest in Spiritualism will be piqued enough that you will study it further, visit a Spiritualist church, and discover its immeasurable value as I have.

I was taught that to converse with spirits of "the dead" is black magic and demonic. "A Christian should have nothing to do with Spiritualism", I was told by several Christian church leaders and believers in my lifetime. But in my opinion, this belief is rooted in ignorance of the truth. I will explain in this book how I came to that opinion.

In this book I'll be finding fault with organized religion mainly Christian churches and I'll be questioning the correctness and infallibility of *The Holy Bible*. If you consider those wrong things to do, maybe even sinful things to do in your way of thinking, please proceed with an open mind. God created us with a free will to think and do as we choose. He also gave us intelligence, logic, and the ability to reason. I like to exercise those gifts at times.

I'm a Christian who now considers himself to be a Christian Spiritualist. That doesn't sit well with many of my friends, some of my family, and a lot of other people who believe Spiritualism and Christianity can't go together. But, they can and if a study of the two is approached with an open mind searching for logical truth as I was and still am, a whole new world of hope, comfort, and enlightenment awaits the inquiring student.

For over fifty years the religious beliefs I'd been taught as a child and throughout my early adult years stood firm and unwavering within my heart, mind, and soul. I did not doubt what I believed was true and correct. I wasn't open to even considering anything other than what I'd been taught by the church. The church had given me "blinders" that prevented me from seeing there are other possibilities and that I should, with an open mind, explore them and consider their worth.

Then unexpected events occurring over the past several years of my life started a rumble beneath the foundation of my beliefs that caused me to re-evaluate my thinking and to search for the truth about what I had been taught, where those teachings originated, and just what it is I should believe. Over the past several years, as more and more evidence that I, in those earlier years, had perhaps been taught incorrectly has come to light, that rumble has intensified and has shaken my beliefs severely. I've come to a point where I now have more questions than I have certainty about who we are, why we are here, and where we go after our physical life is over.

Consider this if you would...

Introduction

A loved one has just taken their last breath. Their body has shut down. They are no longer physically alive. They are "dead". What now becomes of them? Is this the end of their existence or is it the beginning of something better for them? Do they no longer exist at all other than as a memory? Are they to be buried in a grave to await a bodily resurrection upon the return of Jesus Christ? (If that's what truly happens, what then becomes of those who, like my father, have been cremated?) Has your loved one's soul, or spirit, just passed over into a "Spirit World"? Does this Spirit World consist of a Heaven and a Hell? Is there possibly a Purgatory as well? Will they spend an eternity in this Spirit World or will they return to Earth someday as another human being or possibly some other lifeform?

Who can say for certain what happens following a physical death? There are so many differing opinions and beliefs that it can easily become too confusing to sort it all out. Maybe it all comes down to one's own beliefs, convictions, faith, hope, and logic.

The Holy Bible says God knows the heart (1 Samuel 16:7). With this in mind, is it then possible for two people to have conflicting beliefs or even be of two different religions, but in the end live together in the same spiritual world because they followed their personal convictions and beliefs faithfully? After all, their heart was right with God wasn't it?

Then again, maybe none of that matters and we all end up in a Spirit World consisting of various "planes" where we exist in spirit form on an appropriate plane according to our behavior while on Earth and our stage of spiritual development or "enlightenment".

There are so many different religions with so many differing beliefs, so many variations of what happens after death, yet each religion believes they are correct and they may even refer to those of another belief as heathens, pagans, the lost, infidels, or as belonging to a cult.

Then there are those who believe there is no Divine Creator or God, we are here merely by chance, and when our body dies, we are dead…no spirit, no afterlife, nothing…the end…that's it…over and done.

I was raised a Protestant Christian, but could never decide whether to believe that upon death we sleep in a grave awaiting the "second coming" of Jesus Christ when "the dead in Christ shall rise" (1 Thessalonians 4:16) or we immediately go to Heaven as did the thief beside Jesus who, while on the cross, asked Jesus to remember him (Luke 23:39-43). After all, didn't Jesus say to the thief, "Today you will be with me in Paradise"?

Does any of this really matter? We can't be certain of what awaits us after our physical body shuts down. There are those who claim they know exactly what becomes of us and are certain they are correct. Some of them state such things because of their strong beliefs and convictions while others say they've experienced death and then returned. But, even these first-hand accounts of a "near-death experience" vary in their accounts of what happens when we die, how we cross over into the spiritual world, who is waiting for us, and what "Heaven" is like. I myself once "experienced death" and was returned to my body to continue living this life. (That's a story I'll tell of later in this book.)

Introduction

I do believe we are eternal beings created by a Divine Spirit who I call God and I believe extraordinary things along with abundant love await us after we complete our physical life on Earth.

In this book, I'd like to share with you some of the things I've learned and some of the experiences I've had in my quest for spiritual development as well as what caused me to become interested in Spiritualism. I discovered Spiritualism by chance, but it has greatly and wonderfully changed my life. I only wish I had found it much earlier in life.

If someone were to ask me, "What is Spiritualism to you?" I'd say, "It's the icing on the cake!" Our Divine Creator, Infinite Intelligence, Mother-Father Spirit, or whatever you may call the One I call God has created each one of us an immortal being presently occupying a physical body. We are souls, or spirits, who never die, but instead exist for eternity. What we call death is merely a transition from this earthly life to our continuing life in the Spirit World.

So, what's the "cake" you may be asking? The cake is the wonderful, peaceful, loving continuation of life that awaits us. We will be reunited with loved ones who passed over before us; loved ones who know and love us still, are even now with us in spirit, and want to communicate with us. And what then is the "icing"? The icing is what Spiritualism offers us now, contact with our passed loved ones before we are with them again after this incarnate life ends. This contact for me has brought immense help, comfort, and hope.

Spiritualism is not about fraudulent psychics and fortunetellers. It's not about communication with demonic spirits as I was taught by other churches. It's about the reason we are here, proof of continued life, and it's about following the Laws of Nature: God's laws. It's something that, if fully understood and practiced by all, would bring peace to our world.

The Christian church introduced me to the Way. Spiritualism has revealed so much more to me about the Spirit.

I started this "Introduction" with a quote by Galileo. I'd like to end it with another of his quotes my son, Justin Williams, a science fiction and fantasy writer, brought to my attention when he read the first chapters of a draft of this book. You'll discover the relevance of this quote as you continue reading this book:

> *But I do not feel obliged to believe that that same God who has endowed us with senses, reason, and intellect has intended to forgo their use and by some other means to give us knowledge which we can attain by them.*
>
> *– Galileo Galilei*

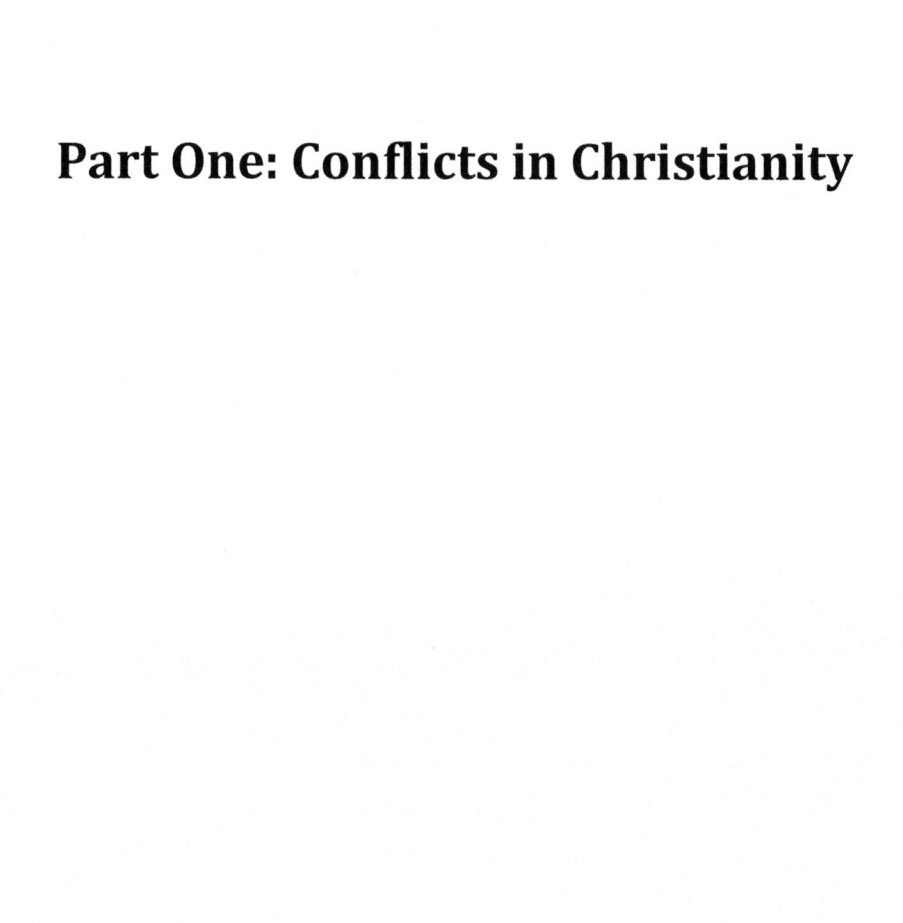

Part One: Conflicts in Christianity

Conflicting Christian Teachings

For God is not the author of confusion, but of peace, as in all churches of the saints - 1 Corinthians 14:33 (KJV)

I started going to church regularly at the age of seven years old. Around that age, or possibly younger, I vaguely remember attending a Mormon church once with a neighbor friend and his family. What stands out in my memory of that experience is the men and the women sat on opposite sides of the church. That's the only church I ever attended that separated the sexes in that manner. There are others I've attended that separate them by what they're allowed to do and say during church services and at church activities. Because the apostle Paul wrote to the church in Corinth telling them, *Let your women keep silence in the churches: for it is not permitted unto them to speak* and *it is a shame for women to speak in the church* (1 Corinthians 14:34-35 KJV), some churches don't allow women to do anything other than serve food at church potlucks, clean up afterwards, and be church custodians. Some churches allow them to teach Bible lessons to the children, but not to an adult class. Other churches ignore this passage considering it "dated and irrelevant" or they interpret it differently and allow the women of their congregation to serve in any way they choose, even as the pastor of the church preaching sermons to the entire congregation including the men.

From age seven through my late twenties, I grew up attending Nazarene churches where I was taught it is a sin to dance and a sin to swim with the opposite sex because dancing and "mixed bathing" break down "the barrier between the two sexes" which promotes sexual promiscuity. It was also a sin to go to movies because of "what goes on in the dark theater or in the cars at the drive-in theater". Or, another reason given me was, "We don't go to movies because it supports the sinful lifestyle of those people in Hollywood who make the movies". Drinking alcohol and smoking tobacco were sinful because "your body is a temple of God so it's sinful to put harmful things into it" plus "it's a bad Christian witness to those watching us". These are just a few of the many "don't dos" determined by the Nazarene church according to their interpretation of *The Holy Bible* and published in their church manual at that time. Back then I thought these ways were to be followed in order to live a life acceptable to God because that is what I had been taught. As I realized later in my life, it was all just the opinion of church leaders based on their own interpretations and convictions.

Their beliefs about Christian lifestyle for some reason changed drastically over the years as I found out when I again attended a Nazarene church and talked with its pastor when I was in my mid-forties. Still no alcohol or tobacco, but dancing, "mixed bathing", and movies were all acceptable. I don't really know why. The pastor only said that over the years things had changed. Their Bible was the same. Maybe they had to change because church attendance was dying. Not many people, especially young people, wanted to follow the Nazarene way when so many other Christian denominations weren't so ridiculously strict in their beliefs and practices.

In the late 1980's, I began attending a Lutheran church. There I completed several "Pastor's Class" sessions to become a member of the church and was taught that all those things the Nazarenes said I couldn't do were quite acceptable to God with the only requirement being moderation of alcohol consumption. There were at least three practices of the Lutheran church (Missouri Synod) I didn't agree with though. In the Nazarene church, during a church service, I could play guitar and sing right up there in front of the congregation. In the Lutheran church, to play guitar wasn't allowed in front of the congregation, but was permitted from the balcony in the back of the sanctuary. Another practice of the Lutheran church, and the main reason I joined the church, was their policy of a "closed communion". You must prove to the pastor you believe as they do in order to take communion in the church. I was newly married to a Lutheran school teacher, but couldn't take communion with her because I was considered "not of like belief" until I completed the Pastor's Class. The third practice I couldn't come to accept was forgiveness of sins by the pastor of the church. During the church service there was recitation by the congregation of a certain prepared traditional reading followed by the pastor's pronouncement that he (not God) forgave us of our sins. The Lutheran church has scriptures to support their beliefs and practices, but many other Christian denominations interpret these scriptures differently or have other scriptures to explain their differences in doctrine.

I've also attended a few Baptist churches. They have no church manual as the Nazarenes had to tell you how to "live right". After attending for a few months the first Baptist church I went to, I asked the pastor for a church manual so I could become more familiar with the Baptist beliefs. I liked that Baptist church very much. He asked me, "What's a church manual?" I explained to him what the Nazarenes had. He then told me the Baptists had no such thing and the church believed we are to live as *The Holy Bible* teaches us and that what's right or wrong in how we live is between God and the individual to determine. It's not the church's place to pass judgement or to dictate. Now, *that* I could easily agree with! Also, they had no required classes for me to complete before I could have communion with the rest of the congregation.

I attended a Pentecostal church for a few months and was taught by a very nice couple through the church's bible study program that God is only to be called, "Jesus", and although I had been baptized in the name of the Father, Son, and Holy Spirit, I had to be baptized again in the name of Jesus in order to make it to Heaven. To their disappointment I passed on that. I feel my one baptism is good enough, thank you.

At the Pentecostal church, as well as at a Foursquare church and an Assembly of God church where I had occasion to play and sing, I heard people "speaking in tongues". When *The Holy Bible* tells of the disciples speaking in tongues (Acts 2:4), were they speaking in foreign languages so others could understand this new gospel they were sent to preach? Or, were they speaking "the language of God" because the Holy Spirit had descended upon them and filled them? I was told by one Assembly of God church member, "If you haven't spoken in tongues, you haven't been filled with the Holy Spirit". There's yet another subject the different Christian denominations can't agree on.

The vast majority of Protestant churches teach that any consumption of alcohol is a sin even though *The Holy Bible* teaches us something different. 1 Timothy 5:23 (KJV) tells us to,

Drink no longer water, but use a little wine for thy stomach's sake and thine often infirmities.

There are churches who teach that God is a trinity, a three-in-one entity consisting of Father, Son, and Holy Spirit. Others believe this isn't possible and that the Father, Son, and Holy Spirit are three separate entities making up one "Godhead".

Some churches teach you are "saved" by faith alone as stated in John 3:16, while others say it is faith plus works that make one worthy of a place in Heaven (James 2:24).

I was taught that Hell is a place of eternal fire and eternal suffering (Matthew 18:8 and 25:46). Another church says God would never allow such a place to exist as He is too loving and Hell is actually a lake of fire where the soul of a sinner is consumed to exist no more (Ezekiel 18:4, Matthew 10:28, and Revelation 20:14-15).

According to Matthew 19:9, Jesus said a man may divorce his wife if she has committed fornication, or adultery. Some call it "biblical grounds" for divorce. Yet a Nazarene minister told me when I was a young man having a decision to make that there are no biblical grounds for divorce and quoted scripture from one of Paul's writings, 1 Corinthians 7:10-11, which says married couples are to stay together.

There are churches in which I cannot serve as a deacon or elder because I have been divorced. These churches use the criteria stated in 1 Timothy 3 when selecting candidates for these positions. The passage includes a verse Paul writes to Timothy saying, *Let the deacons be the husbands of one wife* (1 Timothy

3:12 KJV). I only have one wife. Previous marriages are legally dissolved by the final divorce decree.

"The husbands of one wife", according to the last Protestant Christian church I attended, means no previous marriages regardless of the reason for divorce. Only a man who has been married just once may be considered by the church leaders when choosing candidates to become a deacon or elder. (But, if he is widowed and then remarries, it is accepted as having only one wife.)

Perhaps that church hasn't done their research on the subject. I'm sure the matter has been thoroughly discussed and prayed about by the church leaders who wrote the doctrine, but my research revealed Paul was probably referring to polygamy, not divorce, when he wrote, "husbands of one wife". Although Roman law had already outlawed polygamy at the time, it was still legal in Palestinian Judaism. Jewish oral tradition justified having as many as eighteen wives. Paul may have written "husbands of one wife" because he believed church leaders should not be polygamists. Jesus taught monogamy.

Now, as far as interpreting biblical verses, let me use this as an example of how a person's thinking can go. Here is one possible interpretation of this verse...

"The husbands of one wife" means the deacons and elders must all be married to the same wife – yes, a woman who practices polygamy. The verse doesn't say, "Husbands of one wife each", therefore to me it is saying, "Husbands of only one wife". So, if a church has deacons and elders who have one wife each instead of all being married to the same woman, that doesn't meet the biblical criteria according to what 1 Timothy 3:12 says to me. (I don't actually believe this is what the verse says, but this shows how religious differences arise through varied interpretations of the same biblical passage.)

Some churches do not allow musical instruments to be played in the church nor do they allow special music to be sung such as a gospel quartet or a soloist sharing a song during a church service. One church I've attended practices these restrictions because they claim the early Christians never had instruments or special music in their church meetings. Apparently though, putting a preacher at a pulpit, holding church services in a large building rather than in a home, and incorporating the use of an elaborate modern electric audiovisual system into the service are all okay even though the early Christians did none of these things.

Some churches also believe allowing musical instruments and the singing of special music leads to feelings of pride in those playing and/or singing because of the attention it focuses on them. Evidently telling the preacher his message was inspiring will never create excessive pride, but telling someone who has a God-given gift of musical talent that they play or sing well will lead them astray. So many people who have been blessed with God-given gifts of musical talent are not even able to use their gift to serve Him because of their church's belief. In my lifetime, I've known many pastors, elders, and deacons who let their position in the church corrupt them with pride and self-righteousness. I've seen positions of authority within the church lead to pride much more often than one's sharing their musical talent with the church congregation in worship of their God.

Most Christian denominations hold worship services on Sundays because it was on a Sunday that Jesus was resurrected from the dead. A small number of Christian denominations choose to worship on Saturday because they believe Saturday is the "Sabbath" to be kept holy according to Exodus 20:8, one of the Ten Commandments given by God to the prophet Moses.

There are numerous other differences in beliefs and teachings of the various denominations of the Christian church. I've attended several different Christian denominations during my lifetime each with their own unique doctrine that in some way sets them apart from the other churches. Each denomination believes their way is "the right way". Some even believe their way is the only way acceptable to God for a Christian to be worthy of receiving a reward of eternal life in Heaven.

Since the Christian church as a whole is divided into so many factions which disagree on so many issues, I find it extremely difficult to decide on which church to attend or to even believe any one of these churches can properly guide me in living a Christian lifestyle. If God is not the author of confusion as 1 Corinthians 14:33 tells us, what or who has caused all of this internal conflict and variations of teaching in the Christian church? It all started in the very early church according to the apostles' letters to various churches found in *The Holy Bible* and it has continued and grown throughout the centuries right up to present day.

Perhaps it's wise for a person to either find an all-inclusive church that welcomes diverse beliefs or just to pray and study on their own relying on God to show them the way. God has given us intelligence to learn of Him and He can use our logic and intuition to guide us.

The beliefs and convictions of a church or an individual may cause them to judge the actions and words of others accordingly, but God knows the heart of each person. I believe God will judge us according to our heart. If we strive to live as we are meant to live by always doing what's right, being compassionate and loving, and praying for His guidance and wisdom, God sees and hears that and we are acceptable in His sight regardless of what any church or individual may claim to the contrary.

Is *The Holy Bible* the Infallible Word of God?

All scripture is given by inspiration of God, and is profitable for doctrine, for reproof, for correction, for instruction in righteousness: That the man of God may be perfect, thoroughly furnished unto all good works. - 2 Timothy 3:16-17 (KJV)

Is *The Holy Bible* just a creation of man? Is it the infallible word of God? Or, is it something that falls somewhere between the two? There are biblical scriptures such as 2 Peter 1:19 or 2 Timothy 3:16–17 which can be interpreted to imply it is infallible, but there is no biblical scripture that specifically calls it the infallible word of God. It has been mankind, mainly through written word and sermons preached within the Christian church, who has declared *The Holy Bible* to be the infallible word of God.

If, as is written in 2 Timothy 3:16-17, *all scripture is given by inspiration of God, and is profitable for doctrine*, why then have so many scriptures been omitted from *The Holy Bible* and why are these scriptures never taught or even mentioned in today's Christian churches? Verse 16 of this passage says the scriptures are "inspired of God", not that they are God's infallible word. Verse 17 says, *That the man of God may be perfect, thoroughly furnished unto all good works.* Is it possible for "the man of God" to become "perfect, thoroughly furnished unto all good works" without having read or been taught "all scripture"?

Some claim *The Holy Bible* is infallible because they believe the Holy Spirit gave chosen authors the words to write that became scripture and then also gave to others the direction and wisdom required to assemble *The Holy Bible* as we know it today. But if this is true, why are there so many different versions of *The Holy Bible* and why do the Catholic, the Eastern Orthodox, the Anglican, and the Protestant Bibles differ in what books of scripture are included? The number of books found in the various Christian Bibles range from the 66 books of the Protestant canon to the 81 books of the Ethiopian Orthodox Tewahedo Church canon.

It's clear that books have been subtracted from the Bible over time, but why? Were changes made to settle differences among early Christian sects? Has the highest level of church leadership been molding "God's Word" through the centuries to support their own beliefs and biases? How many changes have been made not by divine inspiration, but simply because man had his own idea of what the world should be?

Evidence of missing books is given in *The Holy Bible* itself. 1 Chronicles 29:29 (KJV) reads: *Now the acts of David the king, first and last, behold, they are written in the book of Samuel the seer, and in the book of Nathan the prophet, and in the book of Gad the seer.* What happened to the books of Nathan and Gad?

I was taught *The Holy Bible* is God's infallible word given directly by God to the authors of the various books within it. I was taught that in order to be a true Christian I must accept the scriptures as they are written without question and to believe every word. I was taught there really are no errors in *The Holy Bible* and those who believe there are contradictions or inconsistencies just misunderstand what they're reading. So, was I taught correctly?

If *The Holy Bible* is truly the word of God, why is there confusion regarding inconsistencies and contradictions? After all, *The Holy Bible* itself says God is not the author of confusion. In 1 Corinthians 14:33 (KJV) it says, *For God is not the author of confusion, but of peace, as in all churches of the saints.* In saying that, wouldn't it leave Satan as the author of confusion? And, confusion exists not only as to whether or not *The Holy Bible* contains inconsistencies and contradictions, but also there is much confusion and debate as to what many scriptures actually mean. This latter element of confusion is the major cause of the numerous sects and denominations found within the Christian religion due to varied interpretations of the same scripture. 1 Corinthians 14:33 tells us that God is the author of peace yet the absence of peace among His believers has divided Christians.

Is *The Holy Bible* truly the word of God or just the words of those incarnate humans who assembled it, translated it, and revised it? Has *The Holy Bible* been corrupted through interpretation and "spinning" of its words and their original meaning to match the beliefs desired to be reinforced by the translators and/or the editors? The various versions of *The Holy Bible* may all be wrong for there can only be one true interpretation. Who is to say which version that is or if it even exists today?

Let *The Holy Bible* and its history speak for itself:

(Before we continue into the history of *The Holy Bible*, please note the word "canon" is used to refer to the books of the Christian Bible. The canonicity of a book, meaning its right to be part of the canon, is dependent upon its recognized authority. The canon of scripture is the result of a collecting together of the various writings which Christians over the centuries have recognized as authoritative. "The Canon" means the list of biblical writings that are used by Christians as the standard by which they evaluate their beliefs.)

The following is a paraphrase of "How the Bible Came to Us" found at The American Bible Society Resources webpage:

(http://bibleresources.americanbible.org/resource/how-the-bible-came-to-us)

> The Bible is a book containing many books written by many authors. "Bible" is a word taken from the Greek word *biblia* which means "books". The books of the Bible were written down over a period of more than eleven hundred years. Many more years passed before the books of the Bible as we know it today were combined into the one book.
>
> Before anything we can now read in the Bible was ever written down, stories of God and His relationship with the people and the rest of His creation were told verbally and were passed down in that manner from one generation to the next. This is what's known as "oral tradition". Oral tradition continued for many generations before the Jewish Scriptures (Old Testament) were written down in a final form.
>
> As societies in the Near East began to develop forms of writing easy enough to learn and use, around 1800 B.C. the traditional stories, songs (or Psalms), and prophecies began to be written down which would later become part of the Bible. These manuscripts were not all written at the same time. The process was completed over centuries of time. As

some books were being written, others continued to be passed along as oral tradition. Since the stories at times came together in a piecemeal fashion and with sometimes more than one version collected, certain parts of the Bible can be confusing.

The original manuscripts of the books of the Bible, both Old Testament and New Testament probably wore out from use or were destroyed centuries ago as they have never been found. However, copies of the original manuscripts were written by scribes and kept in synagogues, churches, and monasteries. Before copies wore out, new copies were made to replace them. As those copies became worn, new copies were made and so on throughout the centuries. Some very old copies are still found preserved in museums and libraries around the world.

It's not known exactly when all of the books of the Jewish Scriptures were finally assembled. Some of these writings may date as far back as 1100 B.C., but it probably wasn't until around 400 B.C. the process of putting the books together began. New books were written as late as the second century B.C. as the earlier works were being collected. The process of deciding which books would become official scripture was often done by Jewish rabbis and continued until almost C.E. 100.

It was during this time the "Septuagint", a Greek translation of the Jewish scriptures, was written. This Greek translation of the scriptures was used by the Greek-speaking Jews scattered throughout the Roman Empire who did not speak Hebrew. The oldest known copies of the Septuagint were written during the second century B.C., more than a hundred years before the birth of Jesus Christ. The main version of the Jewish Scriptures used by the early Christians was the Septuagint.

How it was decided which books were to be included in the Jewish Scriptures is unclear. It is known however that around C.E. 100, a group of Jewish scholars met at Jamnia, a Jewish learning center located west of Jerusalem. The scholars during this time debated which books were to be considered holy enough to be called scripture. The findings of this group of scholars were probably influential in the Jewish community's choice of the thirty-nine books that should be on the holy list. There were seven books, sometimes referred to as the Deuterocanonical books (meaning second list) that were not included on the holy list.

Most Protestant churches of today accept and teach the original list of thirty-nine books as the Old Testament of their Bible. The original thirty-nine books plus the seven Deuterocanonical books make up the Old Testament of the Bibles used by the Roman Catholic, Eastern Orthodox, and Anglican churches.

Jesus Christ and His early followers were Jewish. They used and quoted the Jewish Scriptures. Early stories and sayings of Jesus were passed on orally from about C.E. 30 until about C.E. 60. Then the stories and sayings began to be collected and written down in books called the Gospels which later became part of the New Testament of the Christian Bible. Earlier than the Gospels, some of the letters from the apostle Paul were written to various "churches" (groups of Jesus' followers meeting in homes) scattered throughout the Roman Empire. 1 Thessalonians was probably the first of these letters and may have been written as early as C.E. 50. Other writings now found in the New Testament were written in the late first century or early second century C.E.

The original New Testament books were written in Greek. Greek was the international language of the Roman Empire during this period of time. In the early years of Christianity, these writings were read and passed on as single books or letters. Early Christian church leaders and councils argued for a period of three centuries over which writings should be considered holy and treated with the same respect given to the Septuagint. Finally, in C.E. 367, Athanasius, the bishop of Alexandria, wrote a letter listing twenty-seven books he said Christians should consider authoritative. This list was accepted by the majority of the Christian churches and is the same twenty-seven books in our modern day New Testament.

Greek was the language understood throughout the Mediterranean world when the New Testament books were written, but local languages became popular by the late second century C.E., especially in local churches. The Bible was then translated into Latin, the language of Rome; Coptic, a language of Egypt, and Syriac, a language of Syria.

Pope Damasus I, in C.E. 383, assigned to a scholar-priest, Jerome, the task of creating an official Latin translation of the Bible. Jerome completed the translation of the entire Bible, Old Testament and New Testament, in about twenty-seven years. Jerome's translation became known as the Vulgate and for the next thousand years served as the standard version of the Bible in Western Europe.

In those days and through the Middle Ages, only scholars were able to read and understand Latin. Around the middle of the fifteenth century, the use of vernacular languages was becoming more widespread and acceptable. As more people learned to read, the demand grew for the Bible in those languages. Translators like Martin Luther, William Tyndale, Cassiodoro de Reina, and Giovanni Diodati began to translate the Bible into commonly used languages.

Bible translating continues today. It has been aided by some recent discoveries. Many ancient Greek manuscripts of New Testament books have been discovered over the past one hundred and fifty years. Some very old manuscripts of the Jewish Scriptures were found in 1947 hidden in caves near the Dead Sea in Israel. These manuscripts, now known as the Dead Sea Scrolls, date from the third century B.C. through the first century C.E. and have shed new light on understanding the wording of certain texts allowing for better translations of specific words and verses.

Here's additional information regarding the development of *The Holy Bible* as found at a Wikipedia webpage:

(https://en.wikipedia.org/wiki/Development_of_the_Christian_biblical_canon):

> *The Old Testament (sometimes abbreviated OT) is the first section of the two-part Christian Biblical canon and is based on the Hebrew Bible but can include several Deuterocanonical books or Anagignoskomena depending on the particular Christian denomination.*

Following Jerome's principle of Veritas Hebraica (Latin for "Hebrew truth"), the Protestant Old Testament consists of the same books as the Hebrew Bible, but the order and numbering of the books are different. Protestants number the Old Testament books at 39, while Jews number the same books as 24. This is because Jews consider Samuel, Kings, and Chronicles to form one book each, group the 12 minor prophets into one book, and also consider Ezra and Nehemiah a single book.

The traditional explanation of the development of the Old Testament canon describes two sets of Old Testament books, the protocanonical books and the deuterocanonical books (the latter considered non-canonical by Protestants). According to this theory, certain Church fathers accepted the inclusion of the deuterocanonical books based on their inclusion in the Septuagint (most notably Augustine), while others disputed their status and did not accept them as divinely inspired scripture (most notably Jerome).

The development of the New Testament canon was, like that of the Old Testament, a gradual process.

Irenaeus (died c. 202) quotes and cites 21 books that would end up as part of the New Testament, but does not use Philemon, Hebrews, James, 2 Peter, 3 John and Jude. By the early 3rd century Origen of Alexandria may have been using the same 27 books as in the modern New Testament, though there were still disputes over the canonicity of Hebrews, James, 2 Peter, 2 and 3 John, and Revelation (see also Antilegomena). Likewise by 200 the Muratorian fragment shows that there existed a set of Christian writings somewhat similar to what is now the New Testament, which included four gospels and argued against objections to them. Thus, while there was plenty of discussion in the Early Church over the New Testament canon, the "major" writings were accepted by almost all Christian authorities by the middle of the second century.

The next two hundred years followed a similar process of continual discussion throughout the entire Church, and localized refinements of acceptance. This process was not yet complete at the time of the First Council of Nicaea in 325, though substantial progress had been made by then. Though a list was clearly necessary to fulfill Constantine's commission in 331 of fifty copies of the Bible for the Church at Constantinople, no concrete evidence exists to indicate that it was considered to be a formal canon. In the absence of a canonical list, the resolution of questions would normally have been directed through the see of Constantinople, in consultation with Bishop Eusebius of Caesarea (who was given the commission), and perhaps other bishops who were available locally.

In his Easter letter of 367, Athanasius, Bishop of Alexandria, gave a list of exactly the same books that would formally become the New Testament canon, and he used the word "canonized" (kanonizomena) in regard to them. The first council that accepted the present Catholic canon (the Canon of Trent) may have been the Synod of Hippo Regius in North Africa (393). The acts of this council, however, are lost. A brief summary of the acts was read at and accepted by the Council of Carthage (397) and the Council of Carthage (419). These councils took place under the authority of St. Augustine, who regarded the canon as already closed. Pope Damasus I's Council of Rome in 382, if the Decretum Gelasianum is correctly associated with it, issued a biblical canon identical to that mentioned above, or if not the list is at least a 6th-century compilation claiming a 4th-century imprimatur. Likewise, Damasus's commissioning of the Latin Vulgate edition of the Bible, c. 383, was instrumental in the fixation of the canon in the West. In 405, Pope Innocent I sent a list of the sacred books to a Gallic bishop, Exsuperius of Toulouse. When these bishops and councils spoke on the matter, however, they were not defining something new, but instead "were ratifying what had already become the mind of the church." Thus, from the 5th century onward, the Western Church was unanimous concerning the New Testament canon.

The last book to be accepted universally was the Book of Revelation, though with time all the Eastern Church also agreed. Thus, by the 5th century, both the Western and Eastern churches had come into agreement on the matter of the New Testament canon. The Council of Trent of 1546 reaffirmed that finalization for Catholicism in the wake of the Protestant Reformation. The Thirty-Nine Articles of 1563 for the Church of England and the Westminster Confession of Faith of 1647 for English Calvinism established the official finalizations for those new branches of Christianity in light of the break with Rome. The Synod of Jerusalem of 1672 made no changes to the New Testament canon for any Orthodox, but resolved some questions about some of the minor Old

Testament books for the Greek Orthodox and most other Orthodox jurisdictions (who chose to accept it).

The early church scrutinized a book according to three main factors when deciding if it should be regarded as canonical. These factors were:

1. Authorship – was it written by a recognized prophet, a recognized apostle, or one of their close associates?

2. Truthfulness and Faithfulness – was it generally regarded as authoritative and true by the various congregations of the early church?

3. Soundness – were its teachings consistent with the beliefs of the faith and with the other canonized books?

When choosing which books to canonize, the church leaders did not accept all available scripture and did not arbitrarily select which books to call authoritative. Their final formalized list of books contained those which the early Christian church already considered authoritative based on authorship and content.

Now, let's take a look at the origins of the King James Version of *The Holy Bible*. The King James Version, or KJV, has been the most widely used Bible of English speaking churches for centuries.

The King James Version, also known as the Authorized Version, was not the first English Bible. John Wycliffe made the first known attempt at an English translation of *The Holy Bible* around 1382, but because of this, the 1408 Constitutions of Oxford banned any English translation of the Bible from being written. Later, during the Reformation, William Tyndale began translating the New Testament into English, but was executed before he could complete his project. His work was continued by John Rogers (pseudonym Thomas Matthew) who wrote *Matthew's Bible* in 1537 which had been preceded by *Coverdale's Bible*, an English translation by Miles Coverdale published in 1535 making Coverdale's the first complete English translation of *The Holy Bible*.

In 1538, Henry VIII established The Church of England and called for a universally accepted English Bible. This Bible was a revision of Matthew's Bible and became known as *The Great Bible* or *Whitchurch's Bible*. Later, English Reformation leaders published the *Geneva Bible* in 1560, Anglican bishops authorized the *Bishop's Bible* in 1568, and in 1582, members of the Catholic seminary, English College, in Douai, France, wrote the *Douay-Rheims Bible*, the first officially authorized Catholic Bible translation in English.

In 1603, James VI of Scotland took over the English throne and was crowned King James I of England. At that time, the various English translations of the Bible had created disunity in the kingdom.

The King James Version of *The Holy Bible* was a result of the Hampton Court Conference of 1604. Here, the newly crowned king met with authorities of the Church of England and a few Puritans. King James I wanted to unite the church in England and no longer have the disagreements within the church he inherited.

In 1604, the Geneva Bible was by far the most widely used Bible in England and though the translation was considered accurate, it contained biased notations which were considered to be anti-monarchical and Calvinistic. The other Bibles which had been sanctioned by the Anglican authorities left much to be desired, but they did not contain controversial notations as did the Geneva Bible.

A Puritan, Dr. John Reynolds, president of Corpus Christi College, Oxford, suggested to the king that there be one Bible recognized by the king for universal usage throughout the kingdom. King James I took this idea and ordered a new translation to be written.

When the King James Version was commissioned, there were at least five English versions of the Bible already in circulation. King James I appointed six panels of translators, two meeting at Oxford, two at Cambridge, and two at Westminster to create the King James Version. A total of fifty-four translators began the project in 1604. Of the six panels involved, three oversaw the translation of the Old Testament, two oversaw the translation of the New Testament, and one oversaw the translation of the Apocrypha. The six groups worked independently, and upon completing their work, sent it to the other panels for further comment and revision. The chief members of all six panels then met to make final decisions on all suggested revisions.

The official instructions given to the King James Version translators required them to base their revision on the Bishop's Bible and to consult Tyndale's, Matthew's, Coverdale's, Whitchurch's (The Great Bible), and Geneva Bibles as well. The translation procedure was based upon fifteen rules that were given to the team of fifty-four translators. As examples, the first rule stated: "The ordinary Bible read in the Church, commonly called the Bishops' Bible, [was] to be followed, and as little altered as the truth of the original will permit." The sixth rule demanded that no marginal notes be affixed "but only for the explanation of the Hebrew or Greek words, which cannot without some circumlocution, so briefly and fitly be express'd in the text." Each translator followed all fifteen rules.

Although several preexisting translations contributed to the King James Version, the finished work was very similar to Tyndale's version. A 1998 scholarly analysis concluded that the words of Tyndale account for eighty-four percent of the New Testament and seventy-five percent of the Old Testament books he translated. Evidently there was much more revising than translating done in the creation of the King James Version.

The King James Version then was created not because of a desire to have a new, more accurate translation, but rather as a political compromise for church unity by doing away with the controversial Geneva Bible and the inadequate Anglican versions. The first edition of the King James Version of *The Holy Bible* appeared in 1611.

Additional notes regarding the development of today's Bible:

> During the mid-60's C.E., James, Peter, and Paul were all killed. Their deaths motivated the writing of narratives about the life and words of Jesus Christ as a means to record and preserve the information.
>
> The timing of the writing of the four major gospels (as determined by the majority of researchers) is as follows:
>
> | | |
> |---|---|
> | Matthew | C.E. 80's or 90's |
> | Mark | C.E. 66-70 (the first gospel written) |

Luke   C.E. 80's or 90's

John   C.E. 90-110

Matthew and Luke used Mark's gospel along with "Quelle" (or "QSource") which is a hypothetical collection of sayings that were pre-gospel, primarily the sayings of Jesus Christ, drawn from the early church's oral tradition. Matthew and Luke wrote independently of each other.

The Gospel of Matthew was originally written anonymously. The words, "According to Matthew", were added some time during the second century C.E.

A few interesting things to consider before calling *The Holy Bible* infallible:

The God of the New Testament, the Father of Jesus Christ is a loving, forgiving, peaceful God. *God is love* according to 1 John 4:8 (KJV) and in Romans 13:10 (KJV) we're told, *Love worketh no ill to his neighbour*. Then in 1 Corinthians 13:4-7 (KJV), where love is called "charity", it is defined as,

> *[4] Charity suffereth long, and is kind; charity envieth not; charity vaunteth not itself, is not puffed up,*
>
> *[5] Doth not behave itself unseemly, seeketh not her own, is not easily provoked, thinketh no evil;*
>
> *[6] Rejoiceth not in iniquity, but rejoiceth in the truth;*

> *⁷ Beareth all things, believeth all things, hopeth all things, endureth all things.*

But Jehovah, the God of the Jews and the Old Testament, was a jealous, vengeful, warring God who gave orders to "men of God" to slaughter men, women, and children because of their unbelief. Jehovah ordered His people to murder entire towns and also told them to keep the victims' possessions for themselves. The tenth chapter of the book of Joshua tells of God ordering the slaughter of races of people and following chapters tell of the slaughter and pillage of "enemies" per God's command. 1 Samuel 15 and other Old Testament passages as well tell of additional slaughters ordered by God.

Christians are taught that Moses wrote the first five books of *The Holy Bible*. If Moses did in fact write the first five books contained in the Old Testament, how could he have written in Deuteronomy 34 about his own death?

In Exodus 33:20, God tells Moses that no man can see the face of God and live. According to Genesis 32:30 (KJV), Jacob said, *"...for I have seen God face to face, and my life is preserved"*, but John 1:18 tells us no one has ever seen God except for His only begotten Son, Jesus. So, was Jacob mistaken about who it was he saw? How many others were, as are recorded in *The Holy Bible*, mistaken about their experiences?

In Romans 3:23 (KJV) we read, *For all have sinned, and come short of the glory of God.* But, how can this be true when *The Holy Bible* also tells us Noah and Job were "perfect"? According to Genesis 6:9 (KJV), *Noah was a just man and perfect in his generations, and Noah walked with God.* In Job 1:1 (KJV) we're told, *There was a man in the land of Uz, whose name was Job; and that man was perfect and upright, and one that feared God, and eschewed evil.* Then a few verses later in Job, God Himself when speaking to Satan calls Job perfect. Job 1:8 (KJV), *And the Lord said unto Satan, Hast thou considered my servant Job, that there is none like him in the earth, a perfect and an upright man, one that feareth God, and escheweth evil?* So, if Noah and Job were in fact perfect, Paul's statement in Romans 3:23 is untrue.

Jesus said, according to three of the Gospels, that some of those who heard Him teach would not taste death before He comes again in His kingdom. All of those who heard Jesus teach have long since tasted of death (they have all died). Jesus said this nearly two thousand years ago. (See Matthew 16:28, Mark 9:1, and Luke 9:27.)

In Matthew 12:40 (KJV), Jesus says according to Matthew,

> [40] *For as Jonas was three days and three nights in the whale's belly; so shall the Son of man be three days and three nights in the heart of the earth.*

Three days and three nights? I was taught He was crucified on a Friday (what we now celebrate as "Good Friday") and then was resurrected on a Sunday morning (what we celebrate as Easter). That's three days, but only two nights.

Luke writes in Luke 2:2 regarding the birth of Jesus that Mary and Joseph had to travel to Bethlehem to be counted in a census as decreed by Caesar Augustus in the days when Cyrenius was governor of Syria. The great census carried out by Cyrenius took place in 6 C.E., six years after the birth of Jesus.

Luke, in Luke 1:1-4 (KJV), implies that he felt the writings of the time (which would have included Mark's gospel) contained errors and were incomplete so he, Luke, is therefore, because of his "perfect understanding of things from the start", compelled to write his own version of the gospel to ensure "certainty of those things" which were being taught.

The apostles were forbidden, according to Acts 16:6-8 (KJV), by the Holy Spirit to teach in Asia and not allowed to go to Bithynia:

> *6 Now when they had gone throughout Phrygia and the region of Galatia, and were forbidden of the Holy Ghost to preach the word in Asia,*
>
> *7 After they were come to Mysia, they assayed to go into Bithynia: but the Spirit suffered them not.*
>
> *8 And they passing by Mysia came down to Troas.*

Doesn't this conflict with "the great commission" given by Jesus to His disciples in Mark 16:15 (KJV)? That verse says:

> *15 And he said unto them, Go ye into all the world, and preach the gospel to every creature.*

1 John 4:18 (KJV) tells us,

> [18] *There is no fear in love; but perfect love casteth out fear: because fear hath torment. He that feareth is not made perfect in love.*

Why then does *The Holy Bible* also tell us to both love and fear God? Scriptures teaching us to love God include Deuteronomy 6:5, Matthew 22:37, Mark 12:30, and Luke 10:27. Passages instructing us to fear God include Deuteronomy 6:13, four Psalms, 34:9, 115:13, 128:1, 147:11, three Proverbs, 16:6, 19:23, 22:4, Isaiah 8:13, Luke 12:5, and 1 Peter 2:17. If there is no fear in love and perfect love casts out all fear, how then can we both love God and fear God?

In Galatians 2, Paul writes about certain things Peter had done that Paul says makes Peter dishonest and hypocritical. Hadn't Peter, unlike Paul, actually walked with Jesus and heard His words first hand? Didn't Jesus say to Peter that he, Peter, was the rock upon which the church of Jesus Christ would be built? Was Paul right in saying these things against Peter? Isn't Paul judging Peter which is something Jesus had taught not to be done? Jesus said according to Matthew 7:1 (KJV), *"Judge not, that ye be not judged."*

Early scriptures did not agree on the location where Jesus was born. Matthew wrote it occurred at home. Luke said He was born in a stable. Eusebius, the first ecclesiastical historian, claimed the birth took place in a cave. Constantine erected a temple at that cave to be used for Christian worship. In the apocryphal gospel,

"Protevangelion", James, brother of Jesus, writes that Jesus' birth was in a cave. A cave birth was also believed by Tertullian (220 A.D.) and Jerome (375 A.D.). The Council of Nicea (325 A.D.) decided that the birth of Jesus happened in a stable even though Eusebius was part of that council.

There are many other inconsistencies in *The Holy Bible*. An Internet search will reveal many more than I have presented here although many of those "inconsistencies" that I came across are either misinterpretations or misunderstandings when read in full context. But, many still hold up.

Also very interesting is the discovery of the Dead Sea Scrolls in the late 1940's and the Gnostic writings in *The Nag Hammadi Library* in 1945. These discoveries have caused many traditional Judeo-Christian perceptions to be questioned and/or to further evolve.

On several occasions, I've had a chance to discuss Christianity with an ordained deacon I have known for over thirty years. I'd like to share the text of two emails he wrote to me regarding biblical matters:

> *You already know how I feel about the "Apostle" Paul, but the more I read, the more certain I am that he is exactly the same person Jesus warned would come to discredit the gospel. We both know he contradicted Jesus' teaching on divorce, but here are a few examples of very severe contradictions:*

Jesus says the greatest commandment in the Law is: "'Love the Lord your God with all your heart and with all your soul and with all your mind.' This is the first and greatest commandment. And the second is like it: 'Love your neighbor as yourself.' All the Law and the Prophets hang on these two commandments." (Matthew 22:36-40)

Paul says: "For the entire law is fulfilled in keeping this one command: 'Love your neighbor as yourself'." (Galatians 5:14)

Paul completely removes the command to love God!

Also, Paul is the one that started the tradition of calling church leaders (starting with himself) "Father", which has always rubbed me the wrong way and now I better understand why.

Jesus says: "And do not call anyone on earth 'father,' for you have one Father, and he is in heaven." (Matthew 23:9)

Paul says: "Even if you have ten thousand guardians in Christ, you do not have many fathers; for in Christ Jesus I became your father through the gospel."

These are two pretty big (and blasphemous) contradictions in teaching! There aren't a lot of people I can talk about this with without retribution, so I thought I'd share with you at least!

Also, did you know the Bible never says Mary Magdalene was a prostitute? This has been the teaching I've heard my entire life and it's not even in there. In fact, the

> Eastern Orthodox Church considers her the "apostle to the apostles" because Jesus chose her above all others to be the first to see him after the resurrection. They say she went on many missionary trips with and without Paul and was a great leader in the early church. My studies on her started because our current church is very insistent that women can't be church leaders because of Paul's teachings and I was looking for verses to dispute it. (Paul himself sends a female deacon to deliver his letter to Rome, so he disputes it plenty himself, but people don't like to listen sometimes.)
>
> I ordered a copy of the Nag Hammadi Library book I gave you a while back since I would like to read through it more closely. I found most of those books were excluded from the New Testament because they went against Paul's teachings! If that's the reason, I'm going to reconsider what truth might be inside them. Especially the Gospel of Mary Magdalene!

The second email:

> There are a lot of things that have always bothered me about what the current church teaches. I think a lot of Paul's teachings are the cause for the hypocrisy and division in the church as a whole, and from what I've been told by non-believers over the years, that is exactly what led them away. If Paul's true goal was to destroy what Jesus had started to build, he did an excellent job of it.
>
> I had always thought that Paul was appointed to spread the gospel to the Gentiles, but even that isn't true. Self-

appointed, yes, but that's it. Peter was actually the one who was supposed to do this (Acts 15:7) but Paul seems to have usurped that authority, even going as far as to slander Peter's name in a few of his letters!

All of his authority seems to be self-given based on his "conversion" story. Even that is contradictory, though. The account of it in the first half of Acts says the men with Paul "heard but did not see" when Jesus appeared to Paul, but the second account says they "saw but did not hear." When I look up this contradiction, current church leaders say that one "supplements" the other and they aren't actually contradictory. Sometimes that excuse works, but not here. Opposites cancel, they don't supplement. Also, in all of the Bible, I can't think of another time when an angel, Jesus, or God appeared in some way and people nearby couldn't see or hear. Whenever a holy being came to Earth, everyone in the area saw and was usually afraid. Paul needed witnesses based on Jewish law, but I guess he couldn't get them fully on board with the lie.

I'm very interested to learn more about Mary Magdalene. From what little I've read on her, it's starting to look like she was very important to Jesus, but that early church leaders slandered her because of the views on women of that day (and our current day, for that matter). They didn't want women priests, etc., so they couldn't let it be thought that Jesus himself had a woman in a leadership role. I found a great article about this "frame up" job, and also was interested to read what the Eastern Orthodox Church thinks about her, which is much different than the western churches have taught for centuries. (The Orthodox Church makes it sound like she started our Easter egg tradition, too, which is a fun bit of trivia!)

http://www.uscatholic.org/articles/200806/who-framed-mary-magdalene-27585

https://oca.org/saints/lives/2009/07/22/102070-myrrhbearer-and-equal-of-the-apostles-mary-magdalene

I'll be interested to read what it says about her in the Nag Hammadi books. I believe that she's spoken highly of not only in her Gospel, but in a few of the others, too. That's probably why they weren't considered divinely inspired.

The Council of Nicea is an interesting thing to study. I might do more of that as well. I've always heard that's where they decided the books to include in the modern Bible, but from what little research I've done, there isn't actually any record of that. It is where they decided Jesus was truly God, though, which would lead to the trinity concept. Emperor Constantine did request 50 Bibles be made a few years later, though, so there must have been some decision around that point. Jerome (sainted by the Catholics) supposedly says in an introduction to the Book of Judith that it was included by the Nicene Council to be a sacred scripture, though it obviously isn't included now. Maybe that's because it was written by a woman.

Emperor Constantine presided over the Council, but didn't vote on any matters. Clearly, though, his influence would have been enough in a situation like that. It's also interesting to note that even though we tend to

> *remember him as a Christian emperor, he wasn't actually baptized for over a decade after he convened the council. Maybe he was waiting for the church to be exactly what he wanted before joining up.*
>
> *I've started bringing my Bible to church again and when the preacher preaches, I don't listen, I just read on my own. That "company line" of the church doesn't interest me, and that's all it ever seems to be. We're actually looking around for a new church that is a bit more Jesus-centered, but that tends to be difficult to find. I'd love to find one that ignored Paul's letters, but that's probably impossible!*

Please keep the deacon's last paragraph in mind as we next talk about organized religion and today's Christian church. I find it very interesting that Jesus, in His "Great Commission" told his disciples to preach *the gospel* yet so much of what's preached today in the church comes not from the gospels, but from the Pauline letters. And, although the Christian church has high regard for Paul and he is called a saint, I tend to agree with the deacon that there is reason to doubt the sincerity of Paul. He contradicts Jesus, calls himself "father", and his writings tend to be egotistical and self-centered. Jesus was loving and forgiving. Paul judges, condemns, and invokes his own interpretation and consequent morals and beliefs system into Christianity much like the organized church has done over the centuries. It's no wonder the organized Christian church holds Paul in such high esteem.

Getting back to the claim that *The Holy Bible* is the infallible word of God, I can no longer believe it to be true. Historical inaccuracies, contradictions in recounting events, contradictions in how to live a Christian life, and the numerous translations and versions of *The Holy Bible* including varied book content do not support the claim that it is infallible. Is it inspired by God? I believe much of it probably is or at least originally was, but that doesn't make it perfect and infallible. Mankind's contribution over the centuries has spoiled that possibility. We accept it as the Word of God because we've been taught that it is. But in actuality how much of it really is? And, how much of *The Holy Bible* as we know it today is merely the words of men who over the centuries altered it to prove their beliefs and/or support their goals and desires? Man has ruined the perfection of God's Word just as he ruined the perfection of the Garden of Eden.

Once I realized that my religious education was badly flawed and that *The Holy Bible* was not infallible, I became open to considering other spiritual and religious options and opinions. I also began to question the validity of the church, aka organized religion, as a whole.

Organized Religion and Today's Christian Church

Take heed therefore unto yourselves, and to all the flock, over the which the Holy Ghost hath made you overseers, to feed the church of God, which he hath purchased with his own blood. - Acts 20:28 (KJV)

When I was a teenager, eight of us young people at church formed a singing group. I played guitar, another young man played piano, and there were six girls who did the singing. We weren't together as a group for very long when the piano player informed us he was leaving the group and leaving the church as well. When I asked him why, he replied, "I don't believe in organized religion anymore." Organized religion? I didn't know what that meant and I thought our church was just fine because that was what the church had instilled in me over the nine years I had attended it. I was learning so much there about the right way to live and how to secure eternal life, and most of the friends I spent time with were there at the church. It wasn't until several years later that I came to realize what my friend had meant.

Once I began to see the double-standards of what was taught and expected versus what certain church leaders and major supporters got away with, once I became familiar with the local church politics, once I realized the hypocrisy of so many church members held in high esteem, and once I learned the business side of the church (i.e. income being more important than "soul winning") I began to understand why my friend, after being raised from birth in the church, had changed his opinion of our church and organized religion as a whole.

If Jesus were to once again walk this Earth in this present day, would He commend the leaders of His church for faithfully carrying on His work and spreading His gospel? Or, would He feel towards them as He did the religious leaders of His time incarnate as recorded in Matthew 23?

Has the church become more of a business than a beacon? The church teaches that giving to God (actually it's giving to the church who is supposedly doing "God's work") will be returned multiple times to the giver. Does this happen when you give? Is it just a way to make good Christians "test their faith" by giving more to the church? Does the church make their followers believe they must give more in order to please God?

In my early 20's, I had a job that included handling donations that people from all over the country mailed to a particular megachurch. Numerous donations were received from extremely poor people who stated in letters accompanying their donations that it was the last of what they had and requested prayer that God would provide them with what they needed to pay their bills and feed their family. The church accepting these donations was a Los Angeles based church worth many millions of dollars.

In Matthew 6:19-21 (KJV), Jesus tells us to,

> [19] *Lay not up for yourselves treasures upon earth, where moth and rust doth corrupt, and where thieves break through and steal:*
>
> [20] *But lay up for yourselves treasures in heaven, where neither moth nor rust doth corrupt, and where thieves do not break through nor steal:*
>
> [21] *For where your treasure is, there will your heart be also.*

With this passage in mind, is it right for churches and "men of God" (preachers, etc.) to amass millions of dollars when those supporting them and/or living in their community are barely getting by financially? Should a church spend millions of dollars building, decorating, and maintaining their church building when some of the congregation can barely feed and clothe themselves and their family yet they support the church? Is this what Jesus would do? Is this being charitable? Is this not greed and materialism? Doesn't the church teach that to be materialistic and greedy is sinful? Do they teach that so we will feel guilty about what we have and give more to the church to make them wealthier? What do you think God would rather see mankind do with what He has blessed us with...build massive ornate church buildings and make the pastor a materially wealthy person or instead help those in need? Is it a good Christian witness for a church to flaunt its wealth while homeless are sleeping on the church steps and being told to go elsewhere?

In my mid to late twenties, I attended a church where the pastor once each month had some new project or need that required a special offering to fund because the money needed to pay for it wasn't available in the church budget. He set a monetary goal and asked for the congregation to give marking their contributions to go toward that specific cause. The church congregation was always generous and the goal set by the pastor was always exceeded. He was a fantastic fundraiser. But, he rarely visited the sick or "pastored" his congregation in any other way besides preaching. He was eventually voted out of the church and a new pastor was hired. The church's district office found the terminated pastor a new job as pastor of a church four times the size of our church. He was fired by our church, but then was found a better job with more pay by the district office. I contacted another pastor within the church, a friend of mine who some years earlier had been my youth pastor, and questioned this action by the district office. I asked if it was due to this terminated pastor's ability to raise money that he was given a much larger church. My pastor friend actually got angry with me and told me to never question the church.

When my first marriage failed in my late-twenties and I was going through a divorce, I visited a church where to my surprise many of the people who had attended the church I grew up in were now attending. The associate pastor had been a friend of my older brother and sister at the other church and when he saw me, he was pleased to see me and said that if he'd known I was living nearby he would have been knocking on my door inviting me to come to his church. He invited me to stay for a potluck dinner after church which I did and there this associate pastor introduced me to the church's senior pastor. The senior pastor welcomed me there and talked with me briefly. After telling me how wonderful the associate pastor was and how much his "bus ministry" had grown the church membership the senior pastor asked me questions about my life. When he asked if I was married and I told him I was going through a divorce, he said, "That's too bad", and walked away. He never spoke another word to me. He didn't ask me how I was holding up or if I needed someone to talk to. I guess because I was about to be divorced, he didn't want me around. I didn't go back to that church and no one from that church, not even that associate pastor, ever contacted me after that. A couple of years later it became known that the associate pastor, a married man, was having an extramarital affair with the church organist. He never lost his position and job at the church because of the affair (his bus ministry was too valuable) yet I was written off by that same church because I was going through a divorce for which I had biblical grounds. (The senior pastor never asked me the reason for my divorce.)

Remember that pastor friend of mine that told me to never question the church? He's the same one I mentioned in the first chapter of this book who I talked with regarding divorce. He had told me that there is no such thing as biblical grounds for divorce and if I divorced, I would be sinning. I reminded him of Jesus' words in Matthew 19:9. This minister told me that Paul had written, "Husbands do not leave your wives". I told him I'd take the words of Jesus over those of Paul anytime they were in conflict with each other. After I filed for divorce, he never called me to see how I was even though we had been friends for ten years. I saw him twenty years later when he held a revival at a local Nazarene church. We had lunch the next day and talked about many things. When I reminded him of his advice regarding divorce, he said he didn't recall saying that, but if he had, it was only because he was trying to prevent the divorce.

Back in the late 1970's, one Sunday evening after the church service, I was told by the pastor of the Nazarene church I was attending that the corduroy slacks I had on were not appropriate for church wear. I guess that pastor wasn't familiar with 1 Samuel 16:7. Years later, corduroy slacks and even shorts, T-shirts, and sandals were acceptable attire to the church for any service including the traditionally more formal Sunday morning service.

I've been to churches that ask their congregation to "pledge" an amount of money they'll give to the church for a specific "need of the church", usually to finance a specific project or some "emergency financial need". A church leader, usually the pastor, will stand before the congregation during a Sunday morning worship service and ask for these pledges. Sometimes the names and amounts are written on a board for all the people to see. Other times I've witnessed the pastor ask the congregation to stand and as he names an amount those who will pledge to give that amount are to be seated as the pledge is recorded by the church treasurer. He starts with a high amount and works his way down to a dollar. What happens to those who can only pledge a little or those who can't afford to give and are unable to pledge anything? They're either the last to sit or are left standing in humiliation and embarrassment. After witnessing a few of these pledge sessions, I vowed to walk out anytime such a thing was started again and I did twice before finding a denomination that would never pull such a trick on its people.

The Holy Bible says in Matthew 6:1-4 (KJV) that when you give, do it in secret and in a way such that you "let not thy left hand know what thy right hand doeth". Some say that doesn't apply to church giving, but only applies to giving to the needy. That depends on what version of *The Holy Bible* you consult and/or your interpretation of the passage or your own conviction. By asking for pledges, the church is pressuring each member of the congregation to give because all in attendance at the time can see who pledges and how much they pledge. Is it right for these churches to raise funds in this manner? Isn't the church, via the church leader conducting the pledge session, actually making each member of the attending congregation go against this teaching of Jesus by pledging in front of everyone present how much they will give? 2 Corinthians 9:7 (KJV) says, *Every man according as he purposeth in his heart, so let him give; not grudgingly, or of necessity: for God loveth a cheerful giver.* Another version, the New Living Translation (NLT), says it this way: *You must each decide in your heart how much to give. And don't give reluctantly or in response to pressure. 'For God loves a person who gives cheerfully'.*

I once heard a series of messages from a preacher during a Church of Christ Gospel Meeting that went from a Sunday through a Wednesday. His topic for the series was "The Dream Church". His messages were very judgmental and condemning of a congregation that was not his own. He was the pastor of another Church of Christ church, but was asked to hold the Gospel Meetings at the church I was attending. He blamed the declining church attendance on everyone. When he asked the congregation, "Who is responsible for the decline in church attendance?", first he asked everyone to point at him. Then he said, "Now turn that finger and point to yourself because we are all guilty!" All of us are guilty? He'd never met me or many others in that congregation so what right did he have to say such a thing? Was it because "God had spoken to him" and so he "knew it to be true"? I believe that the vast majority of preachers who "hear from God" are mistaking their subconscious opinion and biased intuition as hearing God's voice. His messages also included other judgmental group condemnations for not giving enough money to the church (a message titled, "Sermon on the Amount") and other messages about how no one in the congregation evangelizes enough, gives enough of their time to the church, reads *The Holy Bible* enough, prays enough, and so on. We were all so unworthy and so inadequate it seemed.

The following Sunday, the local pastor of that same church gave a similarly themed message with his first topic being church attendance. He taught us we should be at church every time the doors are open. He told us that no one claiming to be a Christian has a legitimate excuse to be absent from any church service or activity. I got up and left before the next two topics of our failings were presented. I had heard enough!

I concluded this "dream church" idea that the visiting preacher presented to us was a <u>pastor's</u> dream church because if he had such a church he'd have much less to do himself having more people to delegate to. And, because of the growth of the dream church membership, the church would receive more donations and he could ask for a larger salary. Wouldn't we all like more money for doing less?

As *The Holy Bible* says in 1 Thessalonians 5:17 (KJV), *Pray without ceasing.* I don't have to go to church to commune with God and feel His presence. He is with me wherever I go and I can pray anyplace at any time. *The Holy Bible* says in Hebrews 10:25 not to forsake the assembling of ourselves together. The definition of "forsake" is to quit or leave entirely or to abandon. Choosing to go to church only on a Sunday morning or choosing to only go occasionally to church is not forsaking the assembling. Besides, that verse is not the words of Jesus, but was written most likely by Paul according to tradition. Regular attendance of religious services is a tradition carried over from the Jewish people who attend their synagogues on the Sabbath as a way to keep it holy as per God's commandment.

Jesus never said we have to go to church. He did, however, regularly attend the Jewish synagogue on the Sabbath as Luke tells us in Luke 4:16 (KJV),

> [16] And he came to Nazareth, where he had been brought up: and, as his custom was, he went into the synagogue on the sabbath day, and stood up for to read.

One could argue that although Jesus didn't say we should attend church, we should follow His example of regular attendance. This is a good argument, but to truly follow His example, wouldn't we have to attend a synagogue on the Sabbath? And, what was the main reason Jesus regularly attended the synagogue? Was it to increase His knowledge of the Jewish beliefs and laws? Was it for fellowship with like believers? Or, did He attend in order to keep His Father's commandment which was an Old Testament law?

Early Christians gathered to worship, study, and pray in homes on a Sunday in celebration of Christ's resurrection which occurred on a Sunday. They didn't follow the example set by Jesus.

The pastor of the last Protestant Christian church I attended preached at least three times within one year regarding church attendance. Attendance at his church had been declining. When I attended that church, I only went to the Sunday morning worship services. The pastor there claims there's no good reason for a Christian to not attend church every service. At his church, "every service" includes Sunday morning for Bible study and again for worship service, Sunday night, and Wednesday night.

Apparently, that pastor believes those working at power plants generating the electricity that powers the equipment used during the worship service including the sound system, laptop computer, and projector, as well as the church lighting and HVAC system are all heathens and sinners. I was a power plant technician for 25 years and know firsthand there are many people, Christians included, who for various good reasons have to work on a Sunday to provide for themselves and their families.

As for me attending only Sunday morning church services, I had a very good reason. I feel that church considers me a type of "second-rate Christian". I can never be a deacon or elder because I've been married more than once. I don't meet the church's standards. Every time I attended that church it reminded me of my lower class Christian status as taught and practiced by that denomination. I really don't need to be reminded of that any more often. My past isn't anything I can change, is it?

And, one last thought this one regarding prayer, have you ever attended a church service without someone "leading the congregation in prayer" by praying aloud? To the best of my recollection, I certainly haven't. And, some of those prayers get very lengthy to the point that you see older people sitting down before the prayer ends. Some know better than to even stand up at all! Jesus taught in Matthew 6:5-6 (KJV):

> *⁵And when thou prayest, thou shalt not be as the hypocrites are: for they love to pray standing in the synagogues and in the corners of the streets, that they may be seen of men. Verily I say unto you, They have their reward.*
>
> *⁶But thou, when thou prayest, enter into thy closet, and when thou hast shut thy door, pray to thy Father which is in secret; and thy Father which seeth in secret shall reward thee openly.*

So, since Jesus taught us to pray to God in secret rather than to pray standing in a synagogue or on a street corner, why then do we have people praying aloud during a church service?

Although I have many complaints about organized religion and today's Christian church in general, I still see value in the church as a "launching pad" or introduction into spirituality and the belief in a Divine Being. The messages of a required self-evaluation and repentance along with those messages that encourage a good moral, loving lifestyle striving to be more Godlike through spiritual development can start believers in the right direction.

My various previously described church experiences along with many other occurrences at the churches I have attended and other churches I am familiar with started me thinking new thoughts about how I should actually feel about the importance of organized religion. I became interested in how the Christian church went from humble gatherings in the homes of believers during the first century C.E. to the huge megachurch, multi-million and even multi-billion dollar businesses we have today. (Yes, some religious organizations are worth tens of billions!)

In the books of Acts and Galatians, it is recorded that the first Christian community was centered in Jerusalem with the leaders of the community being the disciples of Jesus namely Peter, James (brother of Jesus), and John (the apostle John not John the Baptist).

I believe it's safe to say the early Christian church was founded by Jesus, following His resurrection, in the city of Jerusalem on the Day of Pentecost (see Acts 2). After His resurrection, Jesus appeared to his apostles and just before ascending to Heaven told His apostles the Holy Spirit would come upon them and empower them to preach the gospel unto the uttermost parts of the world. In Acts 2:1-4 the Holy Spirit descends upon the apostles and empowers them to preach the gospel in the languages of the people who had come from many nations to Jerusalem for the religious celebration.

As a result of the apostles' preaching, about three thousand people repented and were baptized (Acts 2:41). Thus, the church of Jesus Christ, the Christian church, was established in the city of Jerusalem in the year C.E. 33. On every occasion thereafter as the people heard the Gospel of Jesus Christ, believed in Him and repented of their sins, they were "added to the church". The end of the second chapter of Acts tells us, *And the Lord added to the church daily such as should be saved* (Acts 2:47b KJV).

These first Christians, as described in the first chapters of the Acts of the Apostles, were mostly Jews either by birth or conversion. The biblical term "proselyte" is used to refer to the early Christians and historians refer to them as "Jewish Christians".

At first, Christianity was a movement within Judaism. Much of the very early proclamation of Christ's teaching was heard in the Jewish synagogues. When the Jews revolted against Rome beginning in C.E. 66, the Christians did not side with them and by the end of the first century C.E. the Christians had largely separated from the synagogue and began to be recognized as a religion separate from Judaism.

During the first three centuries following the resurrection of Jesus, the early Christian churches were simply Christians meeting in homes. They had no formal church building as we know today. They met to worship in the home of a member of what we would now call the congregation of that church. They had struggles, internal conflicts, and many questions about their new faith as proven by the letters to various churches (the Epistles) included in the New Testament. These conflicts led to division within the early Christian church and sects formed according to the beliefs followed. This was not new to religions for even the Jewish faith during the incarnate life of Jesus had sects. These Jewish sects included the Sadducees, the Pharisees, the Essenes, the Herodians, and a few others.

Some Christian sects believed Jesus' death led to salvation while others believed He never died. Not all sects were monotheists, some believing in as many as thirty gods. For the most part, the early sects have been lost to history, but their existence forced the larger Christian church to confront disputed issues (e.g. the relationship between Jesus and God), define the doctrine to standardize Christianity, and agree on a canonical text that became the New Testament. By the fourth century C.E., most early Christian sects had disappeared.

Beginning around 64 C.E. during the reign of Nero and continuing on until the Edict of Milan in 313 C.E., Christianity was officially regarded as a depraved religion and its practice was illegal in the Roman Empire. The Edict of Milan was a proclamation and political agreement between the Roman emperors, Constantine I and Licinius that permanently established religious toleration for Christianity within the Roman Empire. However, Christianity (as defined by The Council of Nicaea) did not become the official religion of the Roman Empire until the Edict of Thessalonica in 380 C.E.

The Council of Nicaea, 325 C.E., discussed and decided upon many of the important Christian church's traditions and beliefs that the church still follows today. This ecumenical council was organized by the Roman emperor, Constantine I, primarily because he was afraid the disputes within the church at that time would create disorder within his empire. The Council of Nicaea is historically significant as the first effort to attain a consensus of doctrine in the Christian church through an assembly, or council. It was the first occasion where the technical aspects of Christology were discussed. The Council was comprised of bishops representing all of Christianity. The Council decided the relationship between God the Father and Jesus Christ. An agreement was reached on when to celebrate Easter. And perhaps most significantly, from this council came the first uniform Christian doctrine, called The Creed of Nicaea. (The Creed of Nicaea was later developed into what became known as The Nicene Creed by The Council of Constantinople, the second ecumenical council of the church in 381 C.E.)

The Council of Nicaea was the first general council in the history of the Christian church and had significant long-term effects. It was the first time a large group of the bishops of the Church assembled to author a uniformly acceptable doctrinal statement. Also for the first time, the Emperor played a role by assembling the bishops under his authority and using his governmental power to give the council's orders effect. The Council of Nicaea created a precedent for subsequent general councils to adopt creeds and canons. Many of the religious sects that failed to accept the agreed-upon doctrines were regarded as heretical and no longer part of the mainstream Christian church which became Catholicism.

After Constantine Christianized the Roman Empire in the 4th century Christianity became relatively unified. When Christianity became the state religion of the Roman Empire the center of the religion was Byzantium (present-day Istanbul). However, there were different sects that broke away from the mainstream Christian church. The first sects to break from away from Byzantine control were the Egyptian Copts, Syrian Maronites, and Nestorians.

Beginning in the early 16th century, a movement to become known as "The Reformation" ended the relative unity that Christianity had enjoyed for a thousand years under the Roman Catholic Church. The Reformation began in Germany but spread quickly throughout Europe. It was initiated by the German Augustinian monk, Martin Luther, when in 1517 he nailed to a church door in Wittenberg, Saxony, his "Disputation on the Power and Efficacy of Indulgences," a list of questions and propositions for debate, which became known as Luther's "95 Theses". This action by Martin Luther came in response to the growing sense of corruption and administrative abuse in the Catholic Church. It expressed an alternate vision of Christian practice and led to the creation and rise of Protestantism. By the middle of the century, most of north and west Germany had become Protestant.

In England, King Henry VIII, who had been a Catholic, broke with the church and founded the Church of England when the pope refused to grant him a divorce from his first wife, Catherine of Aragon. The Act of Supremacy in 1534 made Henry VIII the head, or "supreme governor", of his newly founded church, a title that would be shared by all future monarchs. John Calvin's *Institutes of the Christian Religion* written in 1536 codified the Church of England doctrines.

Through nearly two thousand years of Christianity the dissention and disagreements continue to grow, creating more and more denominations and factions within the denominations as time passes. A single small town can have several churches of the same denomination. Why are there such differences in beliefs that congregations can't coexist as one? I doubt it's what Jesus would want. Did He fail to make clear what we should believe and how we should live our lives? Or, has the ignorance and at times the greed of man caused all the uncertainty and disagreements that exist in the Christian church as a whole?

The church founded by Jesus Christ which began as small worship groups serving mankind has been corrupted by growing into vast business organizations which do little for mankind when compared to the enormous wealth they've accumulated through misleading and controlling their followers. The simple requirement of believing in Jesus in order to have everlasting life as written in John 3:16 is not enough according to organized religion. Organized religion teaches that you must be faithful in attendance and in support of the church by your giving of time, money, and sometimes even your earthly possessions in order to lead an acceptable Christian life. The combined wealth of these churches, accumulated through the generosity of their followers, could be put to use to help those less fortunate and in need. Instead of giving to those less fortunate as Jesus taught, most churches hoard and accumulate for their own interests.

In all cultures of history even to our present day there are concepts that developed within each group with regards to religion and superstitions. Religions and superstitions are developed through the imagination and inspiration of those individuals who are considered to be the wisest among the population. That doesn't necessarily make their religion and superstitions correct regardless of how strong their faith is or how diligently they practice and hold to their beliefs. So it is today among many religions that claim to be the one true religion, claim to have an infallible divinely-given text to follow, and hold superstitious beliefs regarding spirit communication. Not any one of these is the true religion either.

Consider the very impressive, ornate, lavish churches often found today as well as in the past. The priests and other church leaders dressed in beautifully decorated gowns and headwear. The church choir members all dressed alike in beautiful gowns. From where does all this originate? Is any of this required by biblical scriptures? Did any of the prophets or Jesus and His disciples live this way?

Has Satan corrupted the modern-day churches by destroying the unity of the church and misleading believers into following false doctrines? There is one God, one true way of life, one true interpretation of *The Holy Bible*, yet there are so many variations of beliefs, so many different "Christian" churches, and so many different "Bibles" available. To have unity in religion, all believers must be of the same mind thoughts and convictions with only one Bible containing the same supporting truths.

The vast majority of today's Christians do not follow all of the teachings of *The Holy Bible*. Our next chapter will look at what biblical laws Christians are bound to follow. Rules such as not wearing clothing made of blended fabrics (Leviticus 19:19 and Deuteronomy 22:11) or not marking one's body with tattoos (Leviticus 19:28) and the dietary laws given in Leviticus 11 are rarely followed by Christians or even preached about from the pulpits of churches today.

Christian teaching and practices have evolved over time. The Nazarene church that I grew up attending is a good example of this as I wrote about earlier in this book. Is it right for churches to pick and choose which biblical teachings they will follow? Why do they follow some, but not all?

Usually, these changes come when necessary to save membership and to attract newcomers. Otherwise, the church is doomed to eventually close its doors as members leave or die and younger generations who have no desire to follow what they see as the strict, antiquated laws of that church do not attend. It all comes down to what's necessary to keep the business side (the income) of the church going and growing.

According to a 2007 article available on the website, churchleadership.org, church attendance has been declining for decades. 1980's church membership dropped 10% and in the 1990's it dropped 12%. (It has continued to drop according to more recent reports.) The article also states that about half of all Americans have no "church home". About 1,000 new churches are started each year while around 4,000 churches close their doors and cease to exist. 2.7 million church members a year break from their church and fall into "inactivity" leaving hurt or wounded because of some type of abuse, disillusionment, or neglect. From 1990 to 2000, Protestant church membership in America declined by 5 million even though the population during the same period increased 24 million. In a 2016 Barna "The State of the Church" analysis, 73% of Americans called themselves a Christian and had prayed to God within the past seven days, but only 35% had attended a church service within the past seven days.

The dogmatism of the church, or organized religion, disheartens those in search of true, original Christianity. The church controls its people through the threat of hellfire and damnation. This is why it became organized and promoted in the fourth century C.E. At that time, there was not a strong government and system of law other than religious law, so Constantine created a unified Christian church in order to govern and control his people through the bishops of the church.

Organized religion teaches forgiveness, but judges and condemns those who don't live as the church thinks they should. The church believes only it is right and in creating what's "right" and "wrong" creates divisiveness leading to a feeling of superiority among the church's followers, especially its leaders.

Life is hard enough to live without having the influence of people that lead you astray while causing you to doubt your intuition, abilities, knowledge, and instincts. I listened to too many "wise, Godly people" too many times especially in my youth before I realized they knew much less than they thought they did and their "wisdom" was nothing more than shrouded ignorance.

We have been programmed by the doctrine of organized religion which through the centuries has greatly influenced the laws of man as well as the generally accepted beliefs and consequent thinking of society. This has conditioned our thoughts, limited our mental awareness, and has instilled in us erroneous beliefs which if not realized and re-evaluated will prevent us from allowing ourselves to experience further spiritual awakening and development. Many of us are not making proper use of our intelligence, logic, reasoning, and other God-given abilities. We have let others lead us, mold us, and limit us! Exercise that free will God has given to you. Think for yourself. Draw your own conclusions. Determine for yourself through research, study, prayer, and meditation just what it is that God wants you to believe.

The numerous religions, and sects of each religion, are proof that there are many paths to God and man cannot agree on one specific path. Each person can develop their own spiritual path individually. God gave us free will. The church should not try to control the thoughts of a person and the path that individual must take. The individual should be allowed to independently find their own path to God in their own way and in their own timing.

Out With the Old and In With the New
(Or Should We?)

For as many as are of the works of the law are under the curse: for it is written, Cursed is every one that continueth not in all things which are written in the book of the law to do them. But that no man is justified by the law in the sight of God, it is evident: for, The just shall live by faith. And the law is not of faith: but, The man that doeth them shall live in them. Christ hath redeemed us from the curse of the law, being made a curse for us: for it is written, Cursed is every one that hangeth on a tree: That the blessing of Abraham might come on the Gentiles through Jesus Christ; that we might receive the promise of the Spirit through faith. - Galatians 3:10-14 (KJV)

In a previous chapter, I wrote about the inability of today's Christian churches to agree on what *The Holy Bible* actually says and on how Christians are to conduct themselves in day to day life. Another chapter dealt with the origins of *The Holy Bible*, possible inconsistencies within its pages, and questioned whether or not it is actually the infallible Word of God. There is one more disputed topic within Christianity I'd like to point out before getting into the next chapter. Are Christians subject to Old Testament laws?

Must Christians adhere to Old Testament laws or did the "New Covenant" through the blood of Jesus Christ make the "old covenant" of the Old Testament, the covenant God made with Moses, obsolete? Or, are Christians expected to follow some, but not all of the Old Testament laws? In other words, when it comes to Old Testament laws, are Christians required to follow all of them, some of them, or none of them?

There are two main systems of theology in Christianity, "Covenant Theology" and "Dispensational or New Covenant Theology", the two having opposing viewpoints regarding many things including what to do with Old Testament law.

Covenant Theology believes all old covenant laws still apply unless the next covenant specifically does away with those laws. Dispensational or New Covenant Theology believes all previous laws are superseded by the next covenant unless they are reiterated in that covenant.

If you agree with Covenant Theology you will follow Old Testament and New Testament law. If you agree with Dispensational or New Covenant Theology you will ignore Old Testament law and follow only what the New Testament teaches.

Which theology is correct?

According to Rabbinic Judaism, Moses presented the Old Testament laws to the Jewish people and those laws do not apply to Gentiles, including Christians, except for the Seven Laws of Noah, which it teaches apply to everyone.

The Seven Laws of Noah are:

Out With the Old and In With the New

1. Do not deny God.

2. Do not blaspheme God.

3. Do not murder.

4. Do not engage in illicit sexual relations.

5. Do not steal.

6. Do not eat from a live animal.

7. Establish courts and a legal system to ensure obedience to these laws.

Jesus said, in Matthew 5:17-20 (KJV),

> *[17] Think not that I am come to destroy the law, or the prophets: I am not come to destroy, but to fulfil.*
>
> *[18] For verily I say unto you, Till heaven and earth pass, one jot or one tittle shall in no wise pass from the law, till all be fulfilled.*
>
> *[19] Whosoever therefore shall break one of these least commandments, and shall teach men so, he shall be called the least in the kingdom of heaven: but whosoever shall do and teach them, the same shall be called great in the kingdom of heaven.*
>
> *[20] For I say unto you, That except your righteousness shall exceed the righteousness of the scribes and Pharisees, ye shall in no case enter into the kingdom of heaven.*

However, Jesus did alter a few Old Testament laws:

Exodus 21:24 (KJV) says, *Eye for eye, tooth for tooth, hand for hand, foot for foot.* But, Jesus teaches in Matthew 5:38-39 (KJV), *"Ye have heard that it hath been said, An eye for an eye, and a tooth for a tooth: But I say unto you, That ye resist not evil: but whosoever shall smite thee on thy right cheek, turn to him the other also".*

Deuteronomy 24:1-4 (KJV) says, *When a man hath taken a wife, and married her, and it come to pass that she find no favour in his eyes, because he hath found some uncleanness in her: then let him write her a bill of divorcement, and give it in her hand, and send her out of his house.* But, Jesus teaches in Matthew 5:31-32 (KJV), *"It hath been said, Whosoever shall put away his wife, let him give her a writing of divorcement: But I say unto you, That whosoever shall put away his wife, saving for the cause of fornication, causeth her to commit adultery: and whosoever shall marry her that is divorced committeth adultery."*

Leviticus 19:12 (KJV) says, *And ye shall not swear by my name falsely, neither shalt thou profane the name of thy God: I am the LORD.* And Jesus says in Matthew 5:33-37 (KJV), *"Again, ye have heard that it hath been said by them of old time, Thou shalt not forswear thyself, but shalt perform unto the Lord thine oaths: But I say unto you, Swear not at all; neither by heaven; for it is God's throne: Nor by the earth; for it is his footstool: neither by Jerusalem; for it is the city of the great King. Neither shalt thou swear by thy head, because thou canst not make one hair white or black. But let your communication be,*

> *Yea, yea; Nay, nay: for whatsoever is more than these cometh of evil."*

So, if Jesus did not come to destroy the existing law of the time, why did he change some of them? Those agreeing with the dispensationalists or new covenant followers say that when Jesus said, "I am not come to destroy, but to fulfil", He meant that by sacrificing His life on the cross, He was fulfilling all Old Testament law and prophecies. Here are a few New Testament scriptures to support this:

> Galatians 3:23-25 (KJV):
>
>> *[23] But before faith came, we were kept under the law, shut up unto the faith which should afterwards be revealed.*
>>
>> *[24] Wherefore the law was our schoolmaster to bring us unto Christ, that we might be justified by faith.*
>>
>> *[25] But after that faith is come, we are no longer under a schoolmaster.*
>
> Galatians 3:10-14 (KJV):
>
>> *[10] For as many as are of the works of the law are under the curse: for it is written, Cursed is every one that continueth not in all things which are written in the book of the law to do them.*
>>
>> *[11] But that no man is justified by the law in the sight of God, it is evident: for, The just shall live by faith.*

> ¹² *And the law is not of faith: but, The man that doeth them shall live in them.*
>
> ¹³ *Christ hath redeemed us from the curse of the law, being made a curse for us: for it is written, Cursed is every one that hangeth on a tree:*
>
> ¹⁴ *That the blessing of Abraham might come on the Gentiles through Jesus Christ; that we might receive the promise of the Spirit through faith.*

Romans 10:4 (KJV):

> ⁴ *For Christ is the end of the law for righteousness to every one that believeth.*

Hebrews 8:6 (KJV):

> ⁶ *But now hath he obtained a more excellent ministry, by how much also he is the mediator of a better covenant, which was established upon better promises.*

Hebrews 8:13 (KJV):

> ¹³ *In that he saith, A new covenant, he hath made the first old. Now that which decayeth and waxeth old is ready to vanish away.*

Ephesians 2:15 (KJV):

> ¹⁵ *Having abolished in his flesh the enmity, even the law of commandments contained in ordinances; for to make in himself of twain one new man, so making peace;*

If we must still follow the Old Testament laws, are we to follow them all? And, if not all, but some, which ones? Who decides? Do we not wear clothing made of blended fabrics? Do we wear tassels? Do we stone adulterers? Do we worship on Saturday which is the Sabbath? Do we sacrifice animals to God? Do we refrain from eating "unclean animals"? These are but a few of the many laws given by God according to the Old Testament that for the most part are not followed by Christians today.

From Leviticus 11:8 comes the well-known Jewish law against eating pork. Pigs are considered "unclean and abominable" animals by God according to this scripture. But, Leviticus 11 also names many other unclean and abominable animals. It is written in Leviticus 11:10 (KJV), *And all that have not fins and scales in the seas, and in the rivers, of all that move in the waters, and of any living thing which is in the waters, they shall be an abomination unto you.* All crustaceans and mollusk shellfish have no scales and are therefore unclean. These include shrimp, prawns, lobster, scallops, mussels, oysters, squid, octopus, crabs and other shellfish. If you've eaten any of these, you have violated this law. Ever eaten shark or catfish? According to this verse they, too, are unclean because although they have fins, they have no scales.

Ever trimmed the hair on the side of your head or have you ever trimmed your beard? By doing so you violated Leviticus 19:27 (KJV) which commands, *Ye shall not round the corners of your heads, neither shalt thou mar the corners of thy beard.*

Got a tattoo? Here's one for you, Leviticus 19:28 (KJV), *Ye shall not make any cuttings in your flesh for the dead, nor print any marks upon you: I am the Lord.*

I've attended church on and off for over fifty-five years. Sometimes I attended all four services in a week or more if there were revivals or gospel meetings held. For many years though I was unable to regularly attend because of the rotating shiftwork my job required. Although I've attended churches of several different denominations in my lifetime, I never once heard during any Bible study class or any sermon preached that Christians are exempt from Old Testament laws. Why is that? Have I been going to the wrong churches? *The Holy Bible* does tell us more than once that Christians have a new covenant with God through Jesus Christ doesn't it? The religious leaders of the Jewish people to whom God gave Old Testament laws consider those laws to be theirs alone and not for Christians. So, why can't Christian churches agree on this one? Is it because of the control it gives the church over its followers?

It seems to me the more laws you have to follow according to your church the harder it is to feel you're living a life that pleases God. Consequently, the more unworthy of God's love and forgiveness you will feel. The more unworthy you feel, the more likely you are to attend church to pray, ask forgiveness, and try to make all of your sins and faults right with God. The more you attend church, the more you will be donating of your time and money to the church as you attempt to win God's favor. See the control a church can have over us?

All Old Testament laws other than the Ten Commandments are hearsay. God wrote the Ten Commandments by inscribing them on tablets that He gave to Moses. Exodus 31:18 (KJV) says the Ten Commandments were, "written with the finger of God". All other Old Testament laws were given to the Jewish people by a prophet who claimed to have received them orally from God.

The teachings and commandments spoken by Jesus are direct from the Son of God. Jesus said, *"I and my Father are one"* (John 10:30 KJV). Doesn't this statement made by Jesus mean that His words are God's words? (Any New Testament laws other than those spoken by Jesus are also hearsay. Therefore, ladies, speak up in church if you so desire!)

Many Christians believe the Old Testament is little more than a history of the Jewish people. The laws were given for the people to follow in order for them to prove their love to God. There was no Christ yet with His teaching and His life example to follow as we have today. There was no "John 3:16 promise" for them to put their faith in.

The Ten Commandments can be summed up and followed simply by following the two commandments given by Jesus in Matthew 22:37-40 (KJV):

> *37 Jesus said unto him, Thou shalt love the Lord thy God with all thy heart, and with all thy soul, and with all thy mind.*
>
> *38 This is the first and great commandment.*
>
> *39 And the second is like unto it, Thou shalt love thy neighbour as thyself.*
>
> *40 On these two commandments hang all the law and the prophets.*

In 1 Corinthians 9:20-21 (KJV), Paul speaks of the Jews as being under the law of God, but others, including himself, as being under the law of Jesus Christ:

> *²⁰ And unto the Jews I became as a Jew, that I might gain the Jews; to them that are under the law, as under the law, that I might gain them that are under the law;*
>
> *²¹ To them that are without law, as without law, (being not without law to God, but under the law to Christ,) that I might gain them that are without law.*

Paul sums up "fulfillment of the law" for Christians in Romans 13:9-10 (KJV):

> *⁹ For this, Thou shalt not commit adultery, Thou shalt not kill, Thou shalt not steal, Thou shalt not bear false witness, Thou shalt not covet; and if there be any other commandment, it is briefly comprehended in this saying, namely, Thou shalt love thy neighbour as thyself.*
>
> *¹⁰ Love worketh no ill to his neighbour: therefore love is the fulfilling of the law.*

Christians are not required to keep Old Testament law, the Law of Moses, because those laws were temporary, to be in force only until the Messiah came. Now that He, Jesus Christ, has come and given us a new and better covenant, the old covenant is obsolete.

God has had only one covenant with his people at a time. There are four different covenants found in *The Holy Bible*. These covenants do have differences. An example of one such difference is the foods God permits His people to eat as follows:

1. Adam – Edenic Covenant – Vegetarian foods only

2. Noah – Noahic Covenant – Vegetarian foods plus "clean and unclean" meats

3. Moses – Mosaic Covenant (Old Covenant) – Vegetarian foods plus "clean" meats only

4. Jesus Christ – New Covenant in Christ – Vegetarian foods plus "clean and unclean" meats

The New Covenant through Jesus has replaced the old as we are told in Hebrews 10:9 (KJV):

> *⁹ Then said he, Lo, I come to do thy will, O God. He taketh away the first, that he may establish the second.*

Or, as the New Living Translation (NLT) says in Hebrews 10:9:

> *⁹ Then he said, "Look, I have come to do your will." He cancels the first covenant in order to put the second into effect.*

When we realize that Old Testament laws, though they may still be valid in purpose, are now superseded by the New Covenant in the letter of the law, we are free to accept what Paul implied when he wrote in Colossians 2:16 (KJV):

> *¹⁶ Let no man therefore judge you in meat, or in drink, or in respect of an holyday, or of the new moon, or of the sabbath days.*

We are not required to follow Old Testament law, but instead are to keep the commandments and teachings of Jesus Christ. The Old Testament moral laws, however, can still be useful to Christians as guidelines for holy living.

The Old Testament law forbidding consulting mediums and contact with the dead was a civil law because the penalty for breaking that law was to be cut off from the people (Leviticus 20:6). This was a law for the Jewish nation, not for Christians.

Want another opinion on this matter? Here is something I found on the website, "gotquestions.org":

(https://www.gotquestions.org/Christian-law.html)

> *Question: "Do Christians have to obey the Old Testament law?"*
>
> *Answer: The key to understanding the relationship between the Christian and the Law is knowing that the Old Testament law was given to the nation of Israel, not to Christians. Some of the laws were to reveal to the Israelites how to obey and please God (the Ten Commandments, for example). Some of the laws were to show the Israelites how to worship God and atone for sin (the sacrificial system). Some of the laws were intended to make the Israelites distinct from other nations (the food and clothing rules). None of the Old Testament law is binding on Christians today. When Jesus died on the cross, He put an end to the Old Testament law (Romans 10:4; Galatians 3:23–25; Ephesians 2:15).*
>
> *In place of the Old Testament law, Christians are under the law of Christ (Galatians 6:2), which is to "love the Lord your God with all your heart and with all your soul and with all your mind...and to love your neighbor as yourself" (Matthew 22:37-39). If we obey those two commands, we will be fulfilling all that Christ requires of us: "All the Law and the Prophets hang on these two commandments" (Matthew 22:40). Now, this does not*

mean the Old Testament law is irrelevant today. Many of the commands in the Old Testament law fall into the categories of "loving God" and "loving your neighbor." The Old Testament law can be a good guidepost for knowing how to love God and knowing what goes into loving your neighbor. At the same time, to say that the Old Testament law applies to Christians today is incorrect. The Old Testament law is a unit (James 2:10). Either all of it applies, or none of it applies. If Christ fulfilled some of it, such as the sacrificial system, He fulfilled all of it.

"This is love for God: to obey his commands. And his commands are not burdensome" (1 John 5:3). The Ten Commandments were essentially a summary of the entire Old Testament law. Nine of the Ten Commandments are clearly repeated in the New Testament (all except the command to observe the Sabbath day). Obviously, if we are loving God, we will not be worshipping false gods or bowing down before idols. If we are loving our neighbors, we will not be murdering them, lying to them, committing adultery against them, or coveting what belongs to them. The purpose of the Old Testament law is to convict people of our inability to keep the law and point us to our need for Jesus Christ as Savior (Romans 7:7-9; Galatians 3:24). The Old Testament law was never intended by God to be the universal law for all people for all of time. We are to love God and love our neighbors. If we obey those two commands faithfully, we will be upholding all that God requires of us.

Your opinions and decision regarding Spiritualism may well be determined by how you feel about adherence to Old Testament laws. Were they only for the Jewish people? Are Christians bound by, or free of, Old Testament law? Are the teachings of Jesus Christ a New Covenant of new laws that make Old Testament laws obsolete? Did the teachings of Jesus Christ along with His sacrificial death fulfill and abolish Old Testament law?

The New Testament doesn't prohibit the beliefs and practices found in Spiritualism. I believe the Old Testament law against it is not only hearsay, but because of the New Covenant the law is also obsolete.

Part Two: Seeking Truth in Spiritualism

Message Received Loud and Clear

Beloved, believe not every spirit, but try the spirits whether they are of God: because many false prophets are gone out into the world. - 1 John 4:1 (KJV)

The messages I've received through Spiritualist and Christian Spiritualist mediums have included numerous specific facts known only to me and my passed relative who was the communicating spirit. My receipt of these messages under the circumstances in which I received them has proven to me there is life after death. I cannot believe that these messages, nor the messengers (mediums), are "of the Devil" as I was taught earlier in life. That is the belief held by many Christians I know.

This proof of life after death has made me live a more Christian-like life and also makes me strive to be a better, kinder person. If these spirits and the communication with them is "of the Devil", as so many Christian denominations teach, then why would I want to continue to follow Christ's teachings and strive to be a better person? That isn't what Satan would want me to do.

I have received many messages over the past few years. All of these messages have been received through clairvoyant mediums communicating mentally, or telepathically, with the Spirit World. I have not experienced any other means of mediumship.

Unfortunately, there is no Spiritualist Church close to my home so nearly all of my messages have been received when attending churches in England while visiting family and friends living nearly five thousand miles away from me. The churches I've attended have a guest medium for each service who is invited from a large number of traveling mediums who serve numerous Spiritualist churches. Because of this, there have been many different mediums in England through which I have received messages.

The medium always describes the spirit entity before the message is delivered. The description may include physical characteristics or personality traits known about the spirit while incarnate. There may be mention of an object I have of theirs or an event we shared in the past. In some way the medium proves with whom they are in contact. How could I be so far from home and in the presence of a medium who has never previously heard of me, my passed loved one, or an event or object mentioned and that medium is able to accurately describe physical appearance, personality traits, and other things about my passed loved one along with accurately describing an event or object that is mentioned in the message? And, this has happened to me time after time in various churches hosting various mediums.

Most of the messages I've received have been from my mother and father, but I've even had messages from relatives I never knew of. I'd like to share a number of those messages with you starting with a few from my father.

In one of the first messages I received from my father, he told the medium he never thought while incarnate he'd be able to "communicate like this" with me. He then told the medium regarding me, "He doesn't believe as we do". (At that time I didn't, but was beginning to!) The medium told me my dad said when I feel a cool breeze around me it is proof of him being with me. Immediately I felt a cool breeze like a whirlwind around me. It gave me "goosebumps" on my arms. I told the medium I could already feel a cool breeze. He said, "Yes, that's your dad. He's right there with you now." A lady sitting in the chair next to me said she didn't feel the breeze at all!

I've read that in the Spirit World all knowledge of all things is available to those who wish to study and learn. My father was a self-taught, highly intelligent man. I received a message from him saying that there is much to learn in the Spirit World and he is learning it as fast as possible. He said it is amazing and wonderful.

My dad was a master mariner, a captain in the United States Merchant Marine, with an unlimited master's license allowing him to sail any vessel anywhere in the world. He spent a good portion of his life at sea. During the early years of my life he was gone a lot, but I had a brother who was nine years older than me who sort of stood in for my dad during his absences. A message from my dad came through a medium saying that he was very sorry for not spending more time with me when I was growing up. The medium added that my dad was very emotional about it and was even crying. I can't recall ever seeing my dad cry. I believe that in the spirit world, as we review our life on Earth, there will be many things we feel we could have done differently and been better at. I hope my dad knows I understand that his job kept him away and he has nothing to be sorry for.

Another emotional message from my dad was regarding his two daughters from his first marriage. At a time late in his life he had broken off contact with them. His message to me was that he regrets having broken ties to his daughters. He realized he lost out on a lot by so doing. He suggested I contact his oldest daughter as soon as possible to let her know about his message and his regrets. I did contact my sister right away and she was overjoyed. I had to add my apology to her as well as I had also broken off contact with her and hadn't talked to her in many years. She said that as far as she was concerned, all was good and the past was understood and forgiven. My sister and I are still in contact.

When I was in my late teens through mid-twenties, I worked in a bank. My dad would sometimes call me and ask the lady who directed the incoming calls to tell me it was "Father Williams" calling. Because of that, I started calling my dad, "Father", and did so until he passed over about thirty years later. During a message from my dad, the medium told me that he was saying to her to not tell me it's my dad, but to say, it's my father. That was most definitely my dad!

Now that I'm older, I sometimes tell people that when I look in the mirror I see my dad looking back at me. I don't recognize the reflection as being me because I've aged so much over the years. My dad must have heard me saying this. In one message I received, the medium said, "Your dad is telling me that he is better looking than you are." That was my dad's sense of humor.

An old prayer book and rosary beads were mentioned in another message from my dad. I couldn't think of any prayer book, but I remembered finding rosary beads in his belongings after he passed over and wondered why he had them since he wasn't Catholic. When I told my oldest son about this message, he said, "I have the prayer book. Grandma gave it to me after Grandpa died." Evidently the prayer book and the rosary beads originally were given to my dad as a set during World War II. I gave the rosary beads to my son so the set would remain intact.

Just recently, I was trying to make a very important decision and was hoping for advice through a message. I attended a Christian Spiritualist Church about an eight-hour drive from home hoping to receive a message and I did. My father came through telling the medium that I was contemplating a major decision for which there were only two possible choices, two clearly distinct paths to take, and that there was no right choice to be made as either had its own advantages. It was good to know that either way I decided things would be okay.

I have received several comforting and helpful messages from my mother as well. Often, when I receive a message from her, she brings forward other family members with her who want to send their love and assure me they are together.

I never got to say goodbye to my mother before she died. We lived two thousand miles apart at the time of her passing. She went into the hospital thinking she would be back home in a day or two, but was administered a pain medication in the hospital that never should have been given to an elderly person with asthma. The medication immediately put her into a coma that she never awoke from. I wrote a "goodbye letter" to her which was read at her funeral service. I wondered at the time if my mom was there in spirit hearing the letter being read. Years later, I received a message from her saying she owed me an apology. I told the medium I couldn't imagine anything my mom needed to apologize for. The medium said my mom said she was sorry for not living long enough to say goodbye. That message from my mom removed the regret I had held about my mom's passing without a goodbye from me. I now believe that she was present at her funeral service and did hear my letter as it was read.

In another message from my mom, she said she was sad because since her death her children were no longer close like they were during her incarnate life. She was always glad her children got along so well. Family was her first priority. But, since our mom's death, my half-sister from my mom's first marriage had broken off contact with my younger brother and with me. I told my mom, through the medium, that I would contact my sister. The next month was my sister's birthday so I sent a letter about the message from Mom in a birthday card to her. Three months later I also sent a Christmas card to my sister and her husband. I never received a reply of any kind from my sister for either card. Two years later when wondering if I should do more in trying to reestablish contact with my sister, I received another message from my mom saying I had done all I could and that my sister was being stubborn. My mom asked me to just send "caring thoughts" toward my sister and so I do.

One Mother's Day, my mother and her mother came to me through a medium. My mom told me again she was sorry she didn't get to say goodbye to me. I think this is "code" from my mother to confirm it's her. This was a different medium in a different country than had previously given me messages from my mom. My mom's mother, my grandmother, who I had never known because she passed when my mom was four years old, told me she was sorry we didn't get to know each other, but regardless of that she still loves me very much. She mentioned things from my childhood that told me she had at times seen me and been with me while I was growing up. It was a wonderful experience for me to hear from my mother and maternal grandmother on a Mother's Day.

Shortly after I was forced into an early retirement, I started looking for a "retirement house" something smaller in size, in a different state, and away from industrial plants and a big city. I checked out several locations in various states and had narrowed it down to three. My mom, in a message to me, said she saw me living on a property with a stream running through it. I asked the medium if the stream could be a river as one of the locations I was considering was a town on a river. The medium said "stream" could be a river, so I looked at properties in the town on the river. I came across a listing for a house that was the right size, was in the country not in town, and had a stream running along the back of the property. The property had been listed within two days of my receiving the message from my mom. I put in an offer on the house and am now living there.

After buying the house similar to one described in the message from my mom, I wondered if I had actually bought the right house. A message from my mom a year after moving described the place I had bought and confirmed it was where I should be.

After both our dad and mom had passed, my younger brother and I once had a conversation as to whether or not our parents had actually loved each other. There were many times it seemed they didn't get along very well. A message from my mom sometime after that conversation with my brother confirmed their mutual love and Mom said they were indeed soulmates. That was comforting to know.

Through my studies about Spiritualism and the afterlife, I've learned many believe that spirits have the ability to go wherever they wish to go. This may be true. An uncle of mine, who several times took my younger brother and me to major league baseball games when we were kids, told me through a medium he can now attend any sporting event he wants to.

Another uncle of mine came through with a message for me on another occasion. The medium said, "He is family and has your name, Tom." Actually, I have his name. I was named after him. When the medium asked him his involvement in my life, he said he had been in spirit for a long time and that I was given his name. (He passed over three years before I was born.) The medium said he had ties to the sea and she saw an old Navy uniform. This was all true. My dad and this uncle (a younger brother of my dad's) served together in the Navy in the 1930's to early 40's and were together on the same ship.

The very first message I received was also from an uncle of mine. This is yet another uncle, my dad's youngest brother. He described an arc-flash incident at work that resulted in me receiving first- and second-degree burns over all of my face, neck, arms, and hands. The concussion of the blast gave me a traumatic brain injury which affected my memory and concentration causing me difficulty in performing my job duties. At the time I received the message, about fifteen months after the incident happened, I was on a medical leave from work for evaluation and treatment. I didn't know how things would work out for me regarding future employment and income. The medium said my uncle was telling him everything would be okay. My uncle showed him a black snooker ball and a new broom. The medium said these were very positive signs. As it turned out, I was eventually approved for lifetime disability benefits and no longer had to work 12-hour rotating shifts in an industrial power generation plant. I was forced into an early retirement while in my late fifties and although my income is much less now than when I was employed I now enjoy a better quality of life and much more freedom.

Before my disability benefits had been approved, and during the period I was on medical leave, my employer was pressuring me to go back to work. I wondered if I should return to work or stay on leave to see what would happen. I received a message from my older brother simply saying, "You're doing well". I took that to mean I was on the right course and stayed off work. Later, I was told by a coworker that had I returned to work, my employer had everything in place to fire me. If I had returned to work and been fired, I would have been without any income for over a year. At that time, my disability benefits through my employer would have stopped and the benefits I now receive had not yet been approved.

Sometimes a message from a passed loved one can help you or another incarnate loved one with an ongoing project. Such is the case with a few of the messages I've received.

One of my sons was working on family genealogy when I received a message from someone who gave me his name and said he was family. I told my family about the message, but no one recognized the name. As my son worked further on our ancestry, he came across the name I was given and knew he was following the correct family line.

Another time, I received a message that "George is family". When I told my son about it, he said he had come across a

George in his genealogy research and wondered if he was the ancestor he thought he might be.

One message helped me set straight my relationship to another family member I had known as a child. The medium said to me, "I have a message for you from a relative and I think she's saying her name is Pearl. Do you have a relative named Pearl?" "Yes," I said, "I had an Aunt Pearl on my dad's side of the family." My "Aunt" Pearl said she sees me doing research. That was the message. The research turned out to be researching her true relationship to me. My son's genealogy work showed no Aunt Pearl and after asking an older cousin of mine about Pearl, I discovered that she was actually my dad's cousin who grew up living with my dad and his siblings. She was my second-cousin not my aunt. My parents had always referred to her as "Aunt Pearl".

On another occasion, I received a message from a lady who spelled out her name to the medium and said she just wanted me to know she was a relative. I hadn't heard the name before and didn't know who she was. I later found out that she was my daughter's great-grandmother on her mother's side. I believe she spelled out her name for me because her middle name, though a common name of the era in which she lived, was not spelled as was usually seen.

Sometimes you may receive a message meant to comfort and encourage someone else. A message was given to me through a medium from my daughter's maternal grandfather. He said he was bringing "strong and numerous healing vibes" through with much love and respect. "Someone needs extra healing right now", he said to the medium. That evening as I sat in church and received this message, one of his daughters was in the hospital recovering from surgery and his widow was home with a cast on an ankle she had broken in a recent fall. I passed the message on to those two ladies.

You may sometime receive a message that puts to rest the guilt felt because of a bad choice you made in the past. When having regrets about how I had handled a matter about 25 years earlier that involved my ex-father-in-law who is now passed, I received a message from him saying he now understands those things that had happened while incarnate on Earth. He told me he has a lot of respect for me and that all is good between us. He was a very good man and to receive that message from him means more to me than words could properly express.

The messages I've received from loved ones in spirit have change my life immensely. They have guided me to where I am today away from rotating 12-hour shift work in an industrial plant to a peaceful retired life in the country.

Before receiving my first message, I planned on having to work until I was 70 years old because I thought I wouldn't survive financially without receiving my maximum social security retirement benefit. I had suffered a massive financial loss while in my early fifties that took ninety-five percent of my personal savings and retirement fund. Through messages I received, I was shown a different path, a simpler and more enjoyable lifestyle, and a way to live on less with less and be happier.

Our loved ones in spirit aren't perfect and don't know everything, but they can bring messages of comfort and encouragement and they sometimes can see ahead enough to be of great help to us.

Praying to Die

And this is the confidence that we have in him, that, if we ask any thing according to his will, he heareth us: - 1 John 5:14 (KJV)

You've probably heard the old saying, "Be careful what you wish for. You may just get it." I found it's good to be careful about what you pray for as well. During a period of my life when my dreams and plans fell apart, what I had worked for and accumulated was all lost, and my future seemed hopeless, I prayed asking to die. Life didn't seem to be worth living. I was only around thirty years old at the time, but I didn't feel like starting over.

Within the span of less than one year, I had gone through a divorce, was laid off my job, spent several months looking for a new job, lost my house to voluntary foreclosure, was borrowing a car from my parents, was renting a room to live in at the house of a friend and his wife because I couldn't afford an apartment, and then finally after nearly five months of unemployment I secured a new job that was only an entry-level job and it required I work rotating shiftwork. The job was something I had never wanted to do, but it was a job with security, decent pay, and good benefits.

I had gone from being a district manager of a national leasing company to becoming a trainee refinery process operator. My life's plan of being married once, having an intact nuclear family, a nice house and car, and working at an impressively titled white-collar position was now shattered with some pieces of it impossible to ever recover. I was having an extremely hard time accepting my situation and dealing with so much happening in so little time.

Every night I prayed asking why this had all happened to me. I also prayed every night that I could just go ahead and die.

Early one morning, after several months of praying, my prayer was answered. I awoke when my bed started to shake. I was living in Southern California and having lived my entire life there, I first thought it was an earthquake. I'd experienced many earthquakes in my thirty years of life, but this time was quite different. Before I could get up to go stand in a doorway, I felt my body rising up from the bed. I could see the ceiling coming closer and when I looked down, I saw myself still lying in the bed asleep.

Suddenly, all I could see was a bright white light that had completely surrounded me. All around me was nothing but bright white. I spoke out and asked, "What's going on?" A booming, masculine voice answered, "There are no tomorrows!" I didn't understand what was meant by that and asked, "What?" Again the voice said, "There are no tomorrows!"

I tried to figure out what was happening to me. Had my spirit left my body? Had I died?

Suddenly, I felt a reason to live – my young son who was only about three years old at the time. I shouted out, "No, I can't go. What about my son? He needs me to help care for him." After I spoke these words, I immediately began descending back to my body. The bright white light disappeared and I saw my body as I returned to it.

With my spirit back in my body, I thought, "What was that?" "What just happened?" Then it started again. The bed was shaking and my body felt a strange sensation come over it. It felt like I was starting to rise again. I cried out, "Not again!" and it stopped.

Again I wondered what had just happened. Was it the rapture and I refused to go? I listened a while and heard either my friend or his wife turn in their bed so I knew someone was still there. If it had been the rapture, they would have been taken up, too, I reasoned. Then it hit me. It happened because of my prayer. I had asked to die and had been given the chance to die.

From that day to the present, I never again prayed asking to die. What happened that morning made me realize I do have a purpose in life and reason to live. As life went on, eventually things got much better for me and I came to believe much of what happens in life is for a reason. All I went through that year made me a better person. 1 Thessalonians 5:18 tells us to be thankful in all circumstances and I now say prayers giving thanks to God for what He has brought me through in life. There have been many other trials and challenges in life for me since then, but He has always been there to help me through whatever comes my way.

My "out of body experience" also reinforced my belief that we have a spirit separate from our physical body and that our spirit continues to exist after our physical death occurs.

What Changed My Beliefs?

I didn't believe what was said until I arrived here and saw it with my own eyes. - 1 Kings 10:7a (NLT)

In previous chapters I wrote about many conflicting Christian teachings and reasons they exist, put *The Holy Bible* to the test for infallibility and accuracy, and questioned some of the practices and motives of organized religion. I also admitted the church still has value today as a starting point toward true spiritual enlightenment. I've written here about many of the disheartening experiences I had while attending Protestant Christian churches for over fifty years. I shared many messages I've received through Spiritualist mediums from several of my loved ones who are in spirit and I told of my out-of-body experience.

In this chapter I'd like to further explain why I now add the word "Spiritualist" to who I am. Spiritualism is still relatively new to me and as I continue to become more familiar with it, I find more about it that is in tune with what I had already come to believe. Beliefs I developed through prayer, research, and logical reasoning that are outside the teaching of most Christian churches. I have several reasons for becoming a Christian Spiritualist:

1. The truth in the messages I've received from loved ones in spirit and the circumstances under which I received them.

   Ecclesiastes 12:7 (KJV) says, *Then shall the dust return to the earth as it was: and the spirit shall return unto God who gave it.* Long before attending a Spiritualist church I believed in the eternal existence of my soul, or spirit. But, is it actually possible to communicate with those in spirit? The very first message I received convinced me the spirit lives on after our incarnate life ends and yes, we can have contact with the Spirit World as Spiritualism affirms.

   I was overseas thousands of miles from home at a church where I was not known listening to a medium who had never heard of me or me of him. The message I received through this medium was accurate and detailed. The medium gave me a description of my uncle, even gave me his name. He then proceeded to tell me the message from my uncle and told of objects my uncle was showing him all related to an incident at work I had experienced the previous year. The incident had caused me physical and mental injury and eventually brought major changes to my life. The injuries I sustained were accurately described and future life changes were foretold that came to be within the following two years.

   The many messages I've received since that first one have reinforced my belief in Spiritualism. I've experienced contact with the Spirit World at too many different churches, through too many different mediums, and from too many passed loves ones talking about too many different things for me to not believe it to be true. The messages have been accurate and many times quite detailed. I can't imagine any logical way for it to be fraudulent or merely a string of coincidences.

2. The believability of a Spirit World as Spiritualism teaches versus the Heaven/Hell theory I was taught by Protestant Christian churches.

Even as a child, I had trouble with the concept of a "Hell below". Where is below? Is it in the center of the Earth? If that's where it is it must be jam-packed and overflowing with those trillions or more sinful souls who over the millennia have died and been sent there. And, would a loving Creator God actually be so cruel as to torment one of His creations eternally?

"God is love" ...we hear it said often. *The Holy Bible* confirms it in 1 John 4:8. Many of us believe it to be truth and are very grateful for it. So I ask you to consider, which of the following possibilities makes more sense to you?

Would a loving God, our Divine Creator, sentence your soul to a lake of fire to be consumed or to a Hell of eternal flame and torment?

Or...

Would our loving God instead provide a way for you to repent and redeem your soul once you realized your mistakes and erroneous beliefs?

Doesn't a Spirit World consisting of love, help, and spiritual growth (not destruction or eternal torment) sound like something our loving Creator would provide for us?

Matthew 7:9-11 (KJV) tells us regarding God,

> *⁹ Or what man is there of you, whom if his son ask bread, will he give him a stone?*
>
> *¹⁰ Or if he ask a fish, will he give him a serpent?*
>
> *¹¹ If ye then, being evil, know how to give good gifts unto your children, how much more shall your Father which is in heaven give good things to them that ask him?*

I believe when a soul cries out to God, He will be there to help regardless of at what point in our eternal existence that cry is made.

An Earthly incarnation is so short when compared to eternity. I can't accept that there is no chance for redemption and spiritual growth beyond this life.

To me, the theory of a Spirit World consisting of various planes or levels is more logical and more easily understood and acceptable than the Heaven/Hell theory. There's still a "Hell" in the lowest level of the Spirit World that one creates for oneself because of godless living and beliefs while incarnate, but there is a way to escape that Hell through spiritual awakening and enlightenment. I can also accept and understand there being various levels of "Heaven" to attain as we develop spiritually just as there were various grades we ascended through during our school days as we were taught here during our incarnate life.

3. Spiritualism's belief that a person should be allowed to find their own way to God in their own timing and not be dictated to and controlled by any man-made church doctrine.

One of the "Objects of Spiritualism" is, *To protest against every attempt to compel humanity to worship God in any particular or prescribed manner.* I believe God does not require me to follow any church's doctrine in order to have a heart that is right with Him. There is too much disagreement between the various doctrines of the Protestant Christian churches I attended to know which one, if any, is right.

I remember once while in my late teens a Sunday School teacher asked the class, "What is a sin?" Her definition was, "A sin is anything that comes between you and God." I always remembered her definition and maybe my recollection and further scrutiny of those words later in life were the start of my questioning if what I'd been taught by the church was all correct. If going to a movie theater, or dancing, or doing anything else the church taught as "sin" didn't make me feel separated from God, why would other people feel they are sinning if or when they did them? And, why did some of the other Christian denominations think they weren't sins at all? That's when I started to realize many religious beliefs and practices are personal things for each individual to determine and develop for their self in their own timing with God's help.

I believe that to study and follow the teaching and life of Jesus Christ and the Laws of Nature combined with prayer and meditation will guide you along the right path. Having a loving and just heart and following your heart will make everything right between you and God. I also believe that attending a Spiritualist church and receiving messages greatly helps as well. I've had messages from loved ones saying they're "very pleased with me" and that I'm "doing well". Such messages are very encouraging and comforting to me!

In my lifetime I've witnessed certain things accepted and practiced by some churches that other churches would consider sinful. I realized there isn't any Protestant or Catholic church I would agree with enough to fit in. An all-inclusive church such as a Spiritualist church where all are welcome and accepted is a church I'm comfortable attending.

4. The attitude of certain church leaders and members of the other churches I attended versus the loving reception and acceptance found at the various Spiritualist churches I've attended.

The truth that "God is Love" is more evident in the Spiritualist churches I've attended than in any other church known to me.

As an example, whether I've been married once, twice, or twenty times, the Spiritualist church doesn't judge me, condemn me, or exclude me from anything I know of. What other churches may see as a sin or mistake in one's life is viewed by the Spiritualists as a learning experience resulting in further spiritual development. I can't help but agree with this way of thinking. I know that through failed relationships I have learned valuable lessons that have helped me become a better person. I'm thankful for everything I've been through because of where it has brought me today. I believe things happen for a reason even if we don't realize the good that will come of it at the time. Sometimes what may seem at the time to be a negative event, or series of negative events, is necessary to get you to the positive place in life where you're meant to be.

5. *The Holy Bible* and the doctrine of many organized churches have been manipulated through the centuries to suit mankind's greed and their desire for power and control over the general population.

    Rather than being controlled and dictated to, I prefer to make use of my God-given freewill and intellectual abilities. To do otherwise for me is to show a lack of appreciation for what God has blessed me with.

6. Spiritualism follows the Laws of Nature: God's laws. Spiritualism teaches the same way of life as taught and lived by Jesus Christ.

    Spiritualism has no complicated, controlling doctrine like many other religions. The beliefs and goals of Spiritualism are expressed in two short lists, their

"Declaration of Principles" and "Objects of Spiritualism". (We'll look over those lists in a later chapter.)

Should I Believe What Spiritualism Teaches?

Spiritualism is the religion, science, and philosophy of continuous life based upon demonstrated evidence that the spirits of the so-called dead survive their incarnate life and are able to and do communicate with those incarnate by means of mediumship through a person (a medium) whose organism is sensitive to their vibrations.

The Old Testament laws, as given to the Jewish people by God through Moses, prohibited the consultation of mediums. One such verse is found in Leviticus 19:31 (KJV):

> *^{31} Regard not them that have familiar spirits, neither seek after wizards, to be defiled by them: I am the Lord your God.*

The Old Testament also records that Saul was killed because of his unfaithfulness to God which included a visit to a medium for advice according to 1 Chronicles 10:13 (KJV):

> *^{13} So Saul died for his transgression which he committed against the Lord, even against the word of the Lord, which he kept not, and also for asking counsel of one that had a familiar spirit, to enquire of it;*

However, since we now are only bound by the laws of the New Covenant as is taught by the New Testament and are not required to adhere to the Old Testament law given to the Jewish people, I find no reason why Spiritualism would not be acceptable to God. Jesus never mentioned communication with the dead or familiar spirits and the New Testament doesn't include anything negative about Spiritualism or consulting mediums.

One New Testament passage, Galatians 5:19-21, warns against "works of the flesh" including witchcraft, some translations call it sorcery, and those opposed to Spiritualism will quote this scripture. But, in so doing they prove their ignorance. Spiritualism is not witchcraft or sorcery. Witchcraft is a type of sorcery. Sorcery involves the "black arts" such as witchcraft, wizardry, and black magic. Spiritualists do not believe in or practice witchcraft or sorcery.

1 John 4:1-2 (KJV) gives us this advice concerning communication with spirits:

> *Beloved, believe not every spirit, but try the spirits whether they are of God: because many false prophets are gone out into the world.*
>
> *[2] Hereby know ye the Spirit of God: Every spirit that confesseth that Jesus Christ is come in the flesh is of God.*

Spiritualism acknowledges that Jesus came "in the flesh" and recognizes the value of His teaching and life example. Whether I'm attending a Spiritualist church or a Christian Spiritualist church it should be a given that what transpires there is of God. Though God may be referred to as Infinite Intelligence, Divine

Creator Spirit, or by another name, the One they are referring to is the One Christians call God. A Spiritualist medium would not allow a spirit that is demonic into a church service.

God didn't give me freewill and a mind to reason with so I could blindly follow my fellow man without examining and questioning what I'm being taught as "the truth". It is up to me to use the intelligence, logic and reasoning God has blessed me with to decide what truth is according to my mind and heart.

Can one believe in Spiritualism and still believe *The Holy Bible* to be the word of God? Recalling Ecclesiastes 12:7 (KJV) from the last chapter we read,

> *Then shall the dust return to the earth as it was: and the spirit shall return unto God who gave it.*

The Holy Bible says the spirit returns to God, but can we, or at least some of us, actually communicate with those spirits? Matthew 17:3 says Jesus was seen talking with Moses and Elijah. Considering this biblical verse along with others telling of contact with spirits, and based on my own personal experience, the answer is yes, absolutely yes.

The authors and interpreters of *The Holy Bible*, for the most part, did not believe as do modern Spiritualists. Therefore, their writings and interpretations may contradict or otherwise not support certain principles and objects of Spiritualism. But, does that make the Spiritualist wrong? Or, in the case of those strictly following *The Holy Bible* as a whole, adhering to both Old Testament and New Testament law, could it be those non-spiritualist Christians are simply "the blind leading the blind"?

Does *The Holy Bible* include Spiritualism? Many examples of Spiritualism are found there although, depending on the translation, the wording may be different. What's referred to as a seer or prophet in *The Holy Bible* a Spiritualist may call a medium, a miracle is a manifestation, an angel of the Lord is a high spirit, a voice from Heaven is a direct voice, seeing a vision is clairvoyance, familiar spirits are spirits of those known who have passed over.

In 2 Corinthians 12:1-4 (KJV) Paul tells this story:

> *It is not expedient for me doubtless to glory. I will come to visions and revelations of the Lord.*
>
> ² *I knew a man in Christ above fourteen years ago, (whether in the body, I cannot tell; or whether out of the body, I cannot tell: God knoweth;) such an one caught up to the third heaven.*
>
> ³ *And I knew such a man, (whether in the body, or out of the body, I cannot tell: God knoweth;)*
>
> ⁴ *How that he was caught up into paradise, and heard unspeakable words, which it is not lawful for a man to utter.*

This story of Paul's is about an incarnate man being shown Heaven, but Paul doesn't know if the man was in body or out of body when the incident occurred. Here we have confirmation by Paul that out of body experiences are possible. Also, Paul speaks here of a "third heaven". Could this be a reference to levels of the Spirit World? Genesis 1:1 says that God made the heavens (plural according to most Jewish and Christian Bibles) and the earth. (There are some who believe the Earth's atmosphere is the first heaven, outer space is the second heaven, and paradise is the third heaven. Maybe that's what Paul believed.)

Hebrews 12:22-24 (KJV) mentions "spirits of just men made perfect":

> *²² But ye are come unto mount Sion, and unto the city of the living God, the heavenly Jerusalem, and to an innumerable company of angels,*
>
> *²³ To the general assembly and church of the firstborn, which are written in heaven, and to God the Judge of all, and to the spirits of just men made perfect,*
>
> *²⁴ And to Jesus the mediator of the new covenant, and to the blood of sprinkling, that speaketh better things than that of Abel.*

Does this passage confirm the belief that we continue to develop spiritually and eventually become perfect? This passage also mentions "the new covenant" and Jesus as its mediator.

One might see 1 Peter 4:6 (KJV) as confirmation that there is progression of the spirit after death through enlightenment:

> *⁶ For for this cause was the gospel preached also to them that are dead, that they might be judged according to men in the flesh, but live according to God in the spirit.*

In Matthew 17:1-3 (KJV), three of Jesus' disciples witnessed Jesus walking and talking with Moses and Elijah. This is communication with the dead, isn't it?

And after six days Jesus taketh Peter, James, and John his brother, and bringeth them up into an high mountain apart,

² And was transfigured before them: and his face did shine as the sun, and his raiment was white as the light.

³ And, behold, there appeared unto them Moses and Elias talking with him.

What about the biblical passage about a hand that appeared and wrote on a wall? A story told in *The Holy Bible*, Daniel chapter 5, tells of fingers that suddenly appear and write on a wall during a feast a king is having with one thousand of his lords. The king's wise men cannot interpret the writing and Daniel is summoned and tells the king the meaning. Isn't this manifestation and clairvoyance?

Getting to know about Spiritualism can become very confusing. There are many books available that tell about Spiritualism as it has been revealed to each author by passed loved ones, spirit guides, or by out of body experiences. But, even these accounts conflict with each other in many ways. Perhaps this is because so much about Spiritualism is beyond our human comprehension.

The authors of books that I've read on Spiritualism and also on Spiritism include Allan Kardec, Sir Arthur Conan Doyle, Leon Denis, Andrew Jackson Davis, Madam Amanda Valiant, William T. Stead and Estelle Stead, Rev. E. W. Sprague, Uriah Smith, and others. (I've also read the *NSAC Spiritualist Manual* published by the National Spiritualist Association of Churches (NSAC). This manual includes the principles, objects, definitions, explanations, history, and much more about Modern

Spiritualism. I highly recommend the *NSAC Spiritualist Manual* to anyone wishing to learn more about Spiritualism.)

I'm unable to accept and believe everything I've read about Spiritualism. One of the authors whose work I read claims to have been used by Jesus Christ to give us the "true story" of Jesus's life while incarnate on Earth. The author claims that each encounter with Jesus began by Him saying, "I, Jesus Christ of Nazareth and Calvary..." But, was Jesus actually of Nazareth?

According to one of the other books I read and some further research I've done, Nazareth did not exist in Jesus' day and He was not of Nazareth, but was of a Jewish religious group called Nazoreans. At the time Jesus lived as a man on Earth, there were three major Jewish sects, the Pharisees, the Sadducees, and the Essenes. Among the Essenes was a group called the Nazoreans. Mary and Joseph are believed to have been Nazoreans and raised Jesus according to their beliefs and traditions. Other than biblical references to Nazareth there is no recorded history of Nazareth in the first century C.E.

Also, Jesus, as He supposedly "writes through the author", speaks of His virgin birth as being a result of parthenogenesis which He says is something "well known to man". However, my research on parthenogenesis revealed that this type of virgin birth is known to occur only in lower life forms, never in mammals. So, if parthenogenesis isn't possible in mammals, why would Jesus, if He's truly writing through the author, speak of human virgin births as being caused by parthenogenesis?

In the same book, "Jesus" states that the star seen over the stable at the time of his birth was actually a spacecraft transporting "Lord God". Would a spirit, especially God Himself, need a spacecraft?

In another book, the author discredits Spiritualism and claims that all spirits that speak through mediums are evil and are the "Devil's angels". The author claims these evil spirits claim to be passed loved ones, but are instead frauds who cannot accurately predict the future because only divine spirits could do this. In my own personal experience, I have had messages that included at least three predictions of future events that have come true:

> "New broom" - meaning major life changes for me including retirement and an out of state move,

> "Snooker black ball" - representing a win that was the approval of my permanent disability benefits,

> And...

> "Property with a stream" - which described the house I moved to.

I've so far had no messages with predictions that failed to occur.

Those today, as throughout past centuries, who claim spiritualism is "of the Devil" and also believe that all mediums and any communication with the "dead" are demonic could be compared to the Pharisees mentioned in the gospel of Matthew. In Matthew 9:34 (KJV), the Pharisees said of Jesus, *"He casteth out devils through the prince of the devils"*. The Pharisees said this about the One who, according to Christian belief, was the Son of God who by being crucified on a cross sacrificed His life for the atonement of all the sins of mankind including those of the Pharisees.

What causes such doubt? Is it fear of the unknown? Fear of the unexplainable? Is it simply ignorance?

The miracles performed by Jesus were condemned by the local religious leaders of the time, yet those same religious leaders accepted and taught the miracles performed by Moses.

If Spiritualism is demonic, why do the Spiritualist churches I've attended, especially those calling themselves "Christian Spiritualist", sing some of the same familiar hymns found in other Christian hymnals and why do they pray to God? If these churches were demonic, wouldn't they be worshipping Satan?

Perhaps those today who wish to condemn what Spiritualism has to offer are like those of Jesus' day who though they had eyes, ears, and a mind, still could not see, hear, or understand (Matthew 13:13). Our senses must be opened in order to receive. Enlightenment generally will not be offered to those who are not ready to accept or understand it.

When the belief that the Earth is round was first presented, it was ridiculed because the accepted belief was that the Earth was flat. A German philosopher of the 19th century, Arthur Schopenhauer, said that all truth passes through three distinct stages. First, it is ridiculed. Second, it is violently opposed. Third, it is accepted as being self-evident. Modern Spiritualism has been ridiculed and opposed. When investigated honestly and thoroughly, one will find it self-evident.

Throughout the millennia that mankind has existed on this planet, there have been numerous religions that have come and gone. Worship of idols and worship of mythological gods of the Greeks and Romans are some examples. There were those who believed and were certain their beliefs were the truth and their gods existed. What if what you and I believe is wrong or at least is incomplete?

There was a time when people believed that anyone sick or mentally handicapped was in such a condition because of sin and they were possessed by the Devil or by a demon.

Just as science, medicine, and many other things have evolved and improved over time as human knowledge and enlightenment evolves so goes our religious beliefs and practices. We haven't sacrificed any human life to a god of the sun or anything else for some time now as far as I know. Perhaps Spiritualism is just another step in the evolution and improvement of mankind's religion.

According to *The Holy Bible*, the Egyptians tried to destroy the Hebrews. Later in history, the Hebrews and the Romans tried to destroy Christianity. In more recent times since the beginning of Modern Spiritualism the Christian churches, other than the Christian Spiritualists, have been trying to destroy Spiritualism.

The progression of any religion is up to whatever the people are able to comprehend and willing to accept at the time something new is presented or revealed. Examples of an "evolution" of enlightenment where spiritual matters and God's truth are concerned are The Ark of the Covenant, The Ten Commandments, the birth of Jesus Christ, and most recent, the beginning of Modern Spiritualism.

Perhaps our current mainstream religious beliefs are not all there is to learn about our Creator God and our immortal soul. Has your curiosity reached a place where you now think there may be more to know and experience than what you've been taught?

Religions do evolve over the years. Many people have become more spiritual and less religious. Perhaps now is a good time for those interested and ready to receive further enlightenment to consider, study, and experience Spiritualism.

When press briefings are given by the office of the President of the United States, not all available information is shared because the public, in general, cannot comprehend the "big picture". Likewise, Jesus said in Matthew 13:11 it's not meant for man to know all the mysteries of Heaven. When Jesus taught the multitudes, He did so using parables so they could understand what He was teaching them. Jesus taught His disciples straightforwardly because they were more enlightened and able to comprehend His teaching.

Matthew 13:10-15 (KJV) says:

> *[10] And the disciples came, and said unto him, Why speakest thou unto them in parables?*
>
> *[11] He answered and said unto them, Because it is given unto you to know the mysteries of the kingdom of heaven, but to them it is not given.*
>
> *[12] For whosoever hath, to him shall be given, and he shall have more abundance: but whosoever hath not, from him shall be taken away even that he hath.*
>
> *[13] Therefore speak I to them in parables: because they seeing see not; and hearing they hear not, neither do they understand.*

> *14 And in them is fulfilled the prophecy of Esaias, which saith, By hearing ye shall hear, and shall not understand; and seeing ye shall see, and shall not perceive:*
>
> *15 For this people's heart is waxed gross, and their ears are dull of hearing, and their eyes they have closed; lest at any time they should see with their eyes and hear with their ears, and should understand with their heart, and should be converted, and I should heal them.*

Perhaps Jesus chose his disciples because of their enlightenment and psychic abilities. Jesus did not teach them in parables as he did the multitudes that came to hear Him speak. Perhaps the same applies today. Because we have developed spiritually over the millennia, we can now accept Spiritualism because of our greater ability through spiritual maturity to hear and understand as well as see and perceive. The key to receiving enlightenment is to open your senses and exercise your free will.

1 Thessalonians 5:20 (KJV) tells us to *Despise not prophesyings*. To prophesy is to foretell or predict. Predictions I've been told in messages I received from passed loved ones through Spiritualist mediums have come true. I am certainly not going to despise the prophecy or the means by which I received it.

Please keep an open mind and unbiased thoughts as you consider what Spiritualism offers.

The negative teaching of the organized church against communication with spirits along with those fortunetellers and other self-proclaimed psychics who have been proven to be frauds have misled the general public into believing that

Spiritualism can't be true. But, it's been proven to me to be true through my personal experiences.

Paganism was superseded by Christianity because the message of Christianity offered a clear and confident promise of a future life beyond our Earthly existence. For those of us who believe life exists beyond this physical world, the next logical step in the evolution of our religious beliefs is to communicate with that world and allow those who care about us to teach us, guide us, and assure us that the future life that awaits us is a beautiful, loving life in spirit. This is possible with Spiritualism.

We cannot see television or radio waves, but having a receiver designed to recognize and decipher those energy waves allows us to see and listen to what is transmitted. So it is with the Spirit World. We have spirits all around us wanting to communicate with us, but we're unable to see and hear them unless we have developed our ability to do so. Spiritualist mediums are our "receivers" for contact with the Spirit World.

Spiritualism does not teach a grotesque Hell and a Heaven where all sit around all day worshipping and praising God, but instead believes in a Spirit World or Heaven where one continues to develop spiritually to achieve increased enlightenment leading us to a higher plane to place us closer to God. In the Spirit World character is what matters. You may have been a king on Earth, but your character determines where you stand in the Spirit World.

Instead of faith in an afterlife, Spiritualism provides proof that an afterlife awaits us.

I was never before able to find joy in God because the church constantly found fault with me. I was a member of a congregation that according to the church leaders wasn't attending often enough, wasn't giving enough to the church, wasn't doing enough for the church, and wasn't evangelizing enough to bring more people into the church. But, I found that missing joy when I enhanced my Christian beliefs with Spiritualism.

I've found the Spiritualist church is love and acceptance. It doesn't matter what you believe. It doesn't matter what you've done in your past. It doesn't matter what your current church affiliation is or even if you have one. The Spiritualist church welcomes everyone and in every Spiritualist church I've attended I have felt very welcome.

I found out about Spiritualism by accident...or was it? I didn't seek out a Spiritualist church to attend. I didn't even know such churches existed. A series of major events in my life provided me the opportunity to visit England twice a year for many years. My daughter's maternal grandmother who lives in England introduced me to Spiritualism when I attended a church service with her at a church she had attended for over thirty years.

At first, I was uncomfortable hearing members of the congregation receiving messages from passed loved ones through a medium. I didn't know whether to believe it or not and I felt uncomfortable wondering what I would do or what I might be told if the medium had a message for me. But, after attending the church services a few times and after discussing the beliefs of the church with my daughter's grandmother, I soon felt at ease there and soon received the first of many messages that I have received over the past few years.

That "new broom" my uncle showed the medium in the first message I received at a Spiritualist church meant more than a change from employment to retirement, more than a change of homes, it also meant a change in my beliefs, more hope for eternity, and a closer relationship with God.

Should I believe what Spiritualism teaches? So far as there being an afterlife and possible communication with those already there, yes, I should and I do believe in it based on what's been proven to me through my research and personal experience.

Questions and Beliefs

Prove all things; hold fast that which is good. – 1 Thessalonians 5:21 (KJV)

My beliefs are evolving as I study, learn, experience, and analyze all that's occurred in my life present and past. I continue to study Spiritualism because, as with any religion, there is so much to learn and I have yet many questions to be answered. Many of those questions will go unanswered until my time on Earth is over and I pass over to the Spirit World to become further enlightened.

Some of my beliefs are based on messages I've received from passed loved ones through mediums of various Spiritualist churches. As applicable, I'll mention again here briefly some of those messages that I shared in an earlier chapter.

Here are some of the questions I have followed by some of my current beliefs...

Questions:

Is there any really true religion to be found?

Do all religions lead to a "Paradise" or "Heaven"?

Are these places for the afterlife as promised by different religions actually the same place with different names?

Could this Paradise, Heaven, etc., actually be the "Spirit World" as is believed to exist in Spiritualism?

I was taught that Heaven is above and Hell is below. If Hell is below, where is that exactly? Is it in the core of the Earth? Or could "Heaven above" and "Hell below" be references to levels in the Spirit World where "Hell" would be the lowest plane? (God's creation of Heaven and Earth is told of in *The Holy Bible*, Genesis 1:1, but nowhere in the Bible does it say God created Hell.)

Isn't communication with angels of the Lord or spirits of the Lord as written of in *The Holy Bible* communication with the Spirit World?

Though each of the world's religions teaches peace, forgiveness, and love, they have been the cause of intolerance, racism, hatred, death, and even wars. Why has this happened?

Other religions teach stories that are similar to Jesus' death, resurrection, and ascension. In Hinduism, Krishna was crucified, saved from death, and ascended into Heaven when a great light enveloped him and he disappeared into that light. Buddha's last appearance, according to Buddhism was on top of a rock on a mountain in the presence of his followers when a great light surrounded him and he disappeared into that light. The Iranian prophet, Zoroaster (or Zarathustra), is said to have ascended to Heaven at the end of his Earthly career, around 551 B.C. For centuries preceding the Christian era, Egyptians celebrated the resurrection and ascension of Adonius. Many other ancient "masters" and "gods" of the people of the times were said to have been resurrected and ascended as the closing act of their public career. Is Christianity's belief in the death, resurrection,

Questions and Beliefs

and ascension of Jesus Christ actually based on true historical events or is it a belief borrowed from a previous religion?

Is Modern Spiritualism a revelation of the truth of immortality and life after death?

Do we have an eternal life in a Spirit World with our Creator God and our loved ones who have passed from their incarnate life on Earth?

Is this revelation of Modern Spiritualism God's way of compensating for the failure of other religions to teach the real truth, to keep God first, and to keep their followers interested in their faith in God?

Is the universe a playground for the Spirit World? The planets must serve some purpose.

Could life currently exist on all planets, but because of the limits of our perception we cannot see it or prove it?

Are karma and reincarnation real?

Was reincarnation taught and believed back in biblical times? Matthew 16:13-14 (KJV) seems to suggest that it was:

> *[13] When Jesus came into the coasts of Caesarea Philippi, he asked his disciples, saying, Whom do men say that I the Son of man am?*
>
> *[14] And they said, Some say that thou art John the Baptist: some, Elias; and others, Jeremias, or one of the prophets.*

In Acts 12:11-16 (KJV) people thought when Peter knocked on their door that it must be his spirit. They thought he had died in prison. Isn't that believing in the possibility of a manifestation of a spirit as believed possible by many Spiritualists?

> [11] And when Peter was come to himself, he said, Now I know of a surety, that the Lord hath sent his angel, and hath delivered me out of the hand of Herod, and from all the expectation of the people of the Jews.
>
> [12] And when he had considered the thing, he came to the house of Mary the mother of John, whose surname was Mark; where many were gathered together praying.
>
> [13] And as Peter knocked at the door of the gate, a damsel came to hearken, named Rhoda.
>
> [14] And when she knew Peter's voice, she opened not the gate for gladness, but ran in, and told how Peter stood before the gate.
>
> [15] And they said unto her, Thou art mad. But she constantly affirmed that it was even so. Then said they, It is his angel.
>
> [16] But Peter continued knocking: and when they had opened the door, and saw him, they were astonished.

According to Acts 21:8-12 (KJV), Phillip had four daughters that prophesied. Does this mean they were mediums? And in the same passage, Agabus tells Paul ahead of time of his capture. Is Agabus also a medium? Here's the passage:

> [8] And the next day we that were of Paul's company departed, and came unto Caesarea: and we entered into the house of Philip the evangelist, which was one of the seven; and abode with him.

> ⁹ *And the same man had four daughters, virgins, which did prophesy.*
>
> ¹⁰ *And as we tarried there many days, there came down from Judaea a certain prophet, named Agabus.*
>
> ¹¹ *And when he was come unto us, he took Paul's girdle, and bound his own hands and feet, and said, Thus saith the Holy Ghost, So shall the Jews at Jerusalem bind the man that owneth this girdle, and shall deliver him into the hands of the Gentiles.*
>
> ¹² *And when we heard these things, both we, and they of that place, besought him not to go up to Jerusalem.*

The prophecy told by Agabus regarding Paul's capture later comes true in Acts 22:24-30 (KJV):

> ²⁴ *The chief captain commanded him to be brought into the castle, and bade that he should be examined by scourging; that he might know wherefore they cried so against him.*
>
> ²⁵ *And as they bound him with thongs, Paul said unto the centurion that stood by, Is it lawful for you to scourge a man that is a Roman, and uncondemned?*
>
> ²⁶ *When the centurion heard that, he went and told the chief captain, saying, Take heed what thou doest: for this man is a Roman.*
>
> ²⁷ *Then the chief captain came, and said unto him, Tell me, art thou a Roman? He said, Yea.*

> *²⁸ And the chief captain answered, With a great sum obtained I this freedom. And Paul said, But I was free born.*
>
> *²⁹ Then straightway they departed from him which should have examined him: and the chief captain also was afraid, after he knew that he was a Roman, and because he had bound him.*
>
> *³⁰ On the morrow, because he would have known the certainty wherefore he was accused of the Jews, he loosed him from his bands, and commanded the chief priests and all their council to appear, and brought Paul down, and set him before them.*

Is it wrong to pray to a saint? Isn't that just asking for help from a disembodied spirit? Is praying to a saint a form of worshipping that saint?

Many Christians believe that after human death the body waits to be resurrected just as Jesus was resurrected. So, does the Spirit World contain the souls of those bodies awaiting the second coming of Christ? Why couldn't that be possible? Do we actually wait for a bodily resurrection at Christ's return?

Aren't there also Christians who believe Jesus descended into Hell before his body was resurrected? Jesus said to the thief on the cross next to Him that on that day, the day of his death, he would be with Him in Paradise, but Jesus did not go to Paradise until days later, after His resurrection, when He "ascended unto the Father". Where was Jesus until His resurrection? When did He go to Paradise? Did the thief go directly to Paradise? Isn't this all confusing?

Questions and Beliefs

If the body and spirit lay dead in a grave, then can we believe John 3:16 which states that if you believe in Jesus Christ you have eternal life? "Eternal life" is continuous and without an end. Our bodies die, but our soul - our spirit - lives on eternally. Our spirit is the energy that makes us who we are. Energy can be converted to another type of energy, but energy cannot be destroyed.

If energy can be converted, but never destroyed, does God transfer our energy to a newborn baby when we die instead of our spirit living on as our own individuality? If so, there would be no Spirit World of those who have died in body.

If God finished creation in a week's time, were all souls created by then?

Insanity, disease, damaged organs, deformities, loss of sight or hearing, unpleasant deaths...are these punishments for spiritual crimes?

Good health, happiness, business success, general well-being, comfortable living standards, a satisfying life...are these rewards for being truly repentant and becoming a good spirit?

"Only the good die young"...do those who are good early on have less to learn while incarnate? Has their spirit already achieved higher development than those who required longer lives to learn and prove themselves?

Is the biblical God divine and the Supreme Being? Some Spiritualists talk of a "Lord God" who is not "Creator God".

Numerous religions throughout early history prior to the birth of Jesus Christ, and in several countries located on a few different continents, had what they called, a "son of God" who had been conceived of a virgin as Jesus was. As far back as the 6th century B.C., Laozi (or Lao-Tze) founder of Taoism and worshipped as "Supreme Old Lord", was believed to have been born of a virgin. Others in addition to Jesus Christ and Laozi believed to have been born of virgins include Buddha, Abaoji, Mithras, Krishna, and Melchizedek to name a few. Since religions prior to Christianity claim to have a "son of God", an "only begotten son of God", could it be that the Son of God has been reincarnated many times through the ages with Jesus Christ being the last reincarnation? Was each incarnation greater than the previous one in spiritual expression and mastership because through each incarnation He had greater spiritual development?

Is spiritual development God's way of developing us for being in the company of divine spirits? If you are among "the elite" on Earth, would you take your child to a gathering of your kind before they were knowledgeable of how to act and converse properly within your group? Maybe this is why we learn and experience things including a life (or possibly lives) on Earth and why there are, as many Spiritualists believe, several levels or planes to attain in the Spirit World.

If you wanted to build an airplane you might start with a simple glider to see how it worked. If successful, you then might build something sturdier and motorize it. Then you might add controls to it to guide it and then give it a purpose such as transporting an object. You might then enlarge it and add more power so that it could carry cargo or passengers long distances at fast speeds and then develop it even further to journey into the heavens. Although our Creator could have made us perfect to begin with, He chose to create us with a free will and then see how we

Questions and Beliefs

develop and who we become. Doesn't this make us to Him a much more interesting creation than any of His others? And, wouldn't He find great satisfaction when we, having been given free will, gain the experience and knowledge we need to stand in the presence of high spirits and our Creator?

Does the mind control the spirit and the brain control the physical body?

In *The Holy Bible*, Ecclesiastes 9: 5-6 talks about the living will die and when dead will know nothing. How then do spirits know what they know about us and our relationships with those passed?

> *⁵ For the living know that they shall die: but the dead know not any thing, neither have they any more a reward; for the memory of them is forgotten.*
>
> *⁶ Also their love, and their hatred, and their envy, is now perished; neither have they any more a portion for ever in any thing that is done under the sun.*

Joshua 5:13-15 speaks of a military spirit from God who spoke to Joshua. Is this an example of Spiritualism found in *The Holy Bible*?

> *¹³ And it came to pass, when Joshua was by Jericho, that he lifted up his eyes and looked, and, behold, there stood a man over against him with his sword drawn in his hand: and Joshua went unto him, and said unto him, Art thou for us, or for our adversaries?*
>
> *¹⁴ And he said, Nay; but as captain of the host of the Lord am I now come. And Joshua fell on his face to*

the earth, and did worship, and said unto him, What saith my Lord unto his servant?

¹⁵ And the captain of the Lord's host said unto Joshua, Loose thy shoe from off thy foot; for the place whereon thou standest is holy. And Joshua did so.

According to Daniel 10:5-19, Daniel saw a spirit man that others with him couldn't see. More than once he was contacted and the contact left him drained of energy. Was Daniel what we would today call a medium?

⁵ Then I lifted up mine eyes, and looked, and behold a certain man clothed in linen, whose loins were girded with fine gold of Uphaz:

⁶ His body also was like the beryl, and his face as the appearance of lightning, and his eyes as lamps of fire, and his arms and his feet like in colour to polished brass, and the voice of his words like the voice of a multitude.

⁷ And I Daniel alone saw the vision: for the men that were with me saw not the vision; but a great quaking fell upon them, so that they fled to hide themselves.

⁸ Therefore I was left alone, and saw this great vision, and there remained no strength in me: for my comeliness was turned in me into corruption, and I retained no strength.

⁹ Yet heard I the voice of his words: and when I heard the voice of his words, then was I in a deep sleep on my face, and my face toward the ground.

¹⁰ And, behold, an hand touched me, which set me upon my knees and upon the palms of my hands.

¹¹ And he said unto me, O Daniel, a man greatly beloved, understand the words that I speak unto thee, and stand upright: for unto thee am I now sent. And when he had spoken this word unto me, I stood trembling.

¹² Then said he unto me, Fear not, Daniel: for from the first day that thou didst set thine heart to understand, and to chasten thyself before thy God, thy words were heard, and I am come for thy words.

¹³ But the prince of the kingdom of Persia withstood me one and twenty days: but, lo, Michael, one of the chief princes, came to help me; and I remained there with the kings of Persia.

¹⁴ Now I am come to make thee understand what shall befall thy people in the latter days: for yet the vision is for many days.

¹⁵ And when he had spoken such words unto me, I set my face toward the ground, and I became dumb.

¹⁶ And, behold, one like the similitude of the sons of men touched my lips: then I opened my mouth, and spake, and said unto him that stood before me, O my lord, by the vision my sorrows are turned upon me, and I have retained no strength.

¹⁷ For how can the servant of this my lord talk with this my lord? for as for me, straightway there remained no strength in me, neither is there breath left in me.

¹⁸ Then there came again and touched me one like the appearance of a man, and he strengthened me,

> ¹⁹ And said, O man greatly beloved, fear not: peace be unto thee, be strong, yea, be strong. And when he had spoken unto me, I was strengthened, and said, Let my lord speak; for thou hast strengthened me.

In Matthew 11:14, Jesus calls John the Baptist, "Elias who was to come". Elias is Elijah, the Old Testament prophet. By saying this about John, was Jesus telling us there is reincarnation? *The Holy Bible* says that Elijah didn't die, but instead was taken up by God into Heaven by a whirlwind (see 2 Kings 2:1). Did Elijah come back to Earth as John?

John 1:19-23 (KJV) states:

> ¹⁹ And this is the record of John, when the Jews sent priests and Levites from Jerusalem to ask him, Who art thou?
>
> ²⁰ And he confessed, and denied not; but confessed, I am not the Christ.
>
> ²¹ And they asked him, What then? Art thou Elias? And he saith, I am not. Art thou that prophet? And he answered, No.
>
> ²² Then said they unto him, Who art thou? that we may give an answer to them that sent us. What sayest thou of thyself?
>
> ²³ He said, I am the voice of one crying in the wilderness, Make straight the way of the Lord, as said the prophet Esaias.

It is clear from this passage John did not consider himself to be Elijah reincarnated, but rather the one Elijah foretold of who would come to "make straight the way of the Lord". But, those who believe in reincarnation also believe the memory of past lives does not carry over to a present incarnation.

Matthew 11:20-24 (KJV) talks about those who know of, but have rejected Jesus Christ will be worse off at judgment than those who never knew. Does this apply to those who know of, but reject Spiritualism?

> [20] *Then began he to upbraid the cities wherein most of his mighty works were done, because they repented not:*
>
> [21] *Woe unto thee, Chorazin! woe unto thee, Bethsaida! for if the mighty works, which were done in you, had been done in Tyre and Sidon, they would have repented long ago in sackcloth and ashes.*
>
> [22] *But I say unto you, It shall be more tolerable for Tyre and Sidon at the day of judgment, than for you.*
>
> [23] *And thou, Capernaum, which art exalted unto heaven, shalt be brought down to hell: for if the mighty works, which have been done in thee, had been done in Sodom, it would have remained until this day.*
>
> [24] *But I say unto you, That it shall be more tolerable for the land of Sodom in the day of judgment, than for thee.*

After reading this passage, another question arises. If there's only a Heaven and a Hell, how could one sinful town receive more tolerance than another sinful town come judgement day? This could only be true if there are more than two levels to the afterlife. Does this passage prove the existence of a multi-level Spirit World as taught by Spiritualism?

Malachi 4:1-3 talks about the wicked being cast into fire and burned to ashes. Is this what happens to spirits who fail to accept God's ways or is it just something written by a man thousands of years ago? Doesn't this verse conflict with the teaching of eternal torment in a fiery Hell?

> *For, behold, the day cometh, that shall burn as an oven; and all the proud, yea, and all that do wickedly, shall be stubble: and the day that cometh shall burn them up, saith the Lord of hosts, that it shall leave them neither root nor branch.*
>
> *2 But unto you that fear my name shall the Sun of righteousness arise with healing in his wings; and ye shall go forth, and grow up as calves of the stall.*
>
> *3 And ye shall tread down the wicked; for they shall be ashes under the soles of your feet in the day that I shall do this, saith the Lord of hosts.*

Psalm 146:3-4 says at death thoughts perish. How then can spirits tell of things that happened while living in a physical body?

> *3 Put not your trust in princes, nor in the son of man, in whom there is no help.*
>
> *4 His breath goeth forth, he returneth to his earth; in that very day his thoughts perish.*

2 Peter 3:8-9 (KJV) says,

> *8 But, beloved, be not ignorant of this one thing, that one day is with the Lord as a thousand years, and a thousand years as one day.*

> *⁹ The Lord is not slack concerning his promise, as some men count slackness; but is longsuffering to us-ward, not willing that any should perish, but that all should come to repentance.*

Does this passage say that we may have thousands of years to "come to repentance"? If so, it supports the Spiritualists' belief in a multi-level spirit world where those in the lowest level have a chance to repent and redeem themselves.

1 Thessalonians 5:23 speaks of soul, spirit, and body. Are there three parts to a human? Not just body and spirit? Aren't "soul" and "spirit" words for the same thing?

> *²³ And the very God of peace sanctify you wholly; and I pray God your whole spirit and soul and body be preserved blameless unto the coming of our Lord Jesus Christ.*

In Luke 14:26 (KJV) why does Jesus teach hate? Is "hate" the wrong word? Was something lost in the translation?

> *²⁶ If any man come to me, and hate not his father, and mother, and wife, and children, and brethren, and sisters, yea, and his own life also, he cannot be my disciple.*

I had a message through a medium from one the medium described as a young spirit who was lost possibly in childbirth. Does this mean we are created as spirit to be incarnate and then we develop spiritually while incarnate and continue afterwards in the Spirit World? Or, was that just the case of this young spirit? Some Spiritualists believe we live many lives in order to reach our full spiritual potential, but if this was a young spirit it seems this spirit had no previous incarnations.

Beliefs:

To my nearly life-long friend to whom I tried to tell my experiences, but was so closed-minded he said, "Anyone who thinks they can talk to dead people is crazy!", I'd like to point out there are many people who believe people like us are crazy for believing in a God we cannot see. They also believe we're crazy for believing in a "hereafter" and the existence of a Heaven and a Hell that we cannot see. But, I believe in a God because believing in one makes much more sense to me than believing our world and our living in it just happened by chance. I also believe there is a spiritual world that exists and can communicate with us through mediumship. I believe this because of the detailed messages I've received from various mediums, who had never before seen me and knew nothing about me, but were able to give me accurate messages from many of my loved ones who are in spirit. I do not accept Spiritualism as being demonic because the messages I've received are of a loving nature and they have drawn me closer to my Creator and strengthened my belief in His existence and my eternal life.

I believe the Spirit World is "Heaven" and that "Hell" is a state we create for ourselves through our beliefs and actions. I believe this "Hell" is part of the Spirit World and those in it are not lost eternally, but can better themselves and attain "Heaven" through realizing their errors, admitting their wrong doing, repenting it, and receiving enlightenment of spiritual things.

Our spiritual path is basically our "growing up" period. We should not act immaturely, but instead act mature. We are given eyes with which to see, ears with which to hear, and knowledge of the path we should take. Then we are set free to walk that path to God. I believe we should listen to and follow our intuition.

There is enlightenment available to those who are open-minded and do not have "tunnel vision" in regards to spiritual matters. I was taught tunnel vision by the Nazarene church, but through study and especially life experiences I have come to broaden and expand on my beliefs. There is still much enlightenment that awaits my finding it.

There is but one Divine Creator God. This divine spirit has many names according to the many religions of the world. I respect your right to define God differently than I do and to call Him whatever name you choose.

Upon the death of our physical body, our soul, or spirit, passes over into a Spirit World where we will be with our loved ones who have passed over before us. We have a spirit family there. It is something to look forward to. In a message I received from my mother, she brought forward several of my passed family members and then said, "The family is all together".

Thought communication is the closest link between the two worlds.

We are spirits experiencing a temporary human life.

Our incarnate life is our classroom for learning what we came to learn.

There is a much bigger overall picture and larger purpose than most people realize for what we go through in life. It is more than just random occurrences and coincidences. Ultimately everything we experience, everything that happens to us, is for a reason and for our own good as it contributes to our spiritual growth.

Our spirit family is with us and spends time with us. They send their love and encouragement to us through messages we receive via mediums. The medium gives information received from our loved one in spirit to verify to us who it is they're in contact with and to prove the existence of spiritual life after our physical life on Earth. I've had several messages from passed love ones that tell of things they've seen me do. They tell me they are with me and other incarnate family members. They're always with us, just as during that message from my father, the medium told me when I feel a cool breeze it's my father being with me. I felt the breeze immediately giving me "goosebumps" on my arms while the lady sitting in the chair next to me felt nothing.

Our soul's entry into the Spirit World is not waiting for Christ's return. Not only did Jesus tell the thief on the cross beside Him, "Today you will be with me in Paradise", but I've had many messages from my parents, brother, and other loved ones who have passed away and were Christians.

Suicide doesn't send you to "Hell". I've had two messages from an uncle who killed himself after being diagnosed with terminal cancer. He is in the Spirit World with our other family members.

Cremation doesn't keep your spirit from Heaven. My father who was cremated has been the source of many messages for me.

The Spirit World is one of positive energy and love.

The Spirit World is Heaven. All religions and ways of believing will be represented there.

Questions and Beliefs

Heaven, Hell, and Purgatory...maybe these are planes of the Spirit World.

You have a free will. You're not forced to learn anything, but at some point you will want to.

Wisdom is the process of merging life experiences with spiritual growth. Spiritual development determines an individual's wisdom.

"As you sow, so shall you reap" is true in the Spirit World. "As you are, so will you be" is also true.

Do not think any loved ones are lost in Hell for actually they are in the loving, forgiving care of God with an opportunity to be redeemed and may progress from their self-made "Hell" into a "heavenly plane".

In the Spirit World, or "Heaven", we will live in love which is God. After all, Heaven is God's world. We will be free of misery and all other bad things the world gives us as a natural result of the absence of God that we have on Earth.

If your desire is to be with God, then live a life of love for God is love. If you want to go to Heaven, live a life of love.

Our loved ones who are in spirit love us more and more as they grow in grace and in knowledge of God.

The extent to which one loves is a testament of their religion. It's not the church one identifies with. That doesn't matter in the Spirit World. The extent of indifference or hatred one has testifies to that person's lack of religion. It holds back the love that is within the soul. Such a person has much yet to learn spiritually.

A church that promotes indifference, hatred, unacceptance of those who believe differently lacks the love that is God's love. A church such as this is not a true religion of our Creator God.

Our loved ones in spirit long to communicate with us. Too often, we are too busy with the hurried routine of our lives. We need to have some quiet time in prayer, thought, or meditation to allow spirit communication.

Death does not end all. Rather it starts so much more for us when we leave our Earthly bodies. Who we are in this life we continue to be with an eternity to experience God's love without the negative forces of this world acting against us. Once we realize what awaits us in Heaven, we will improve ourselves in this life to better prepare for what eternity will bring. The sooner we learn that God is love, we are created by God, His love dwells within us as our spirit, and we continue a life beyond this life we now know on Earth...once we realize all this and accept it as truth, we will live more harmoniously with our fellow man and with all of God's creation. We will live more, appreciative more, and look forward to our life after this physical life has ceased.

"Death" is a transition rather than a transformation. We leave our body and continue on in a conscious existence. Our mind is clearer and our memory sharper. A change does take place, but it is a change of circumstances not a change in our character. The transition is seamless. We pass immediately from the physical world to the Spirit World and will remain able to see the physical world though we are in spirit.

When your mind is opened up, the work is half done.

The worst evil of present day is one's loss of the soul. If the soul is found, love prevails. If love prevails, we are at peace. This loss of the soul is a result of being too busy. Not taking time to pray, think, meditate, and find your soul. Too much hurrying, too much materialism, too much striving for Earthly things that mean nothing once we leave our Earthly bodies. The soul gets crowded out by our busy lifestyle and our focus on things of the physical world. *For what shall it profit a man, if he shall gain the whole world, and lose his own soul?* – Mark 8:36 (KJV)

Your soul, or spirit, is the part of you that lasts and lives on eternally. Your spirit is the real you. Your spirit is the Divine in you. Your spirit is what communicates with the Spirit World.

God is love and love is God. When you hate or otherwise do not love you are shutting God out of your life. Every time you love, you take a step toward Heaven and God. When you do not love, you are taking steps back and away from Heaven and God.

God is love. Love is God. And, Heaven is the perfect realization of this unity.

In Heaven, as we will it to be, so shall it be. We can be anywhere doing anything just by thinking it or willing it.

The stars and planets of the universe will become very familiar to us in the afterlife. They are the playground for our spirit.

There is so much to learn and know in Heaven that we will develop a passion to learn which will continue to grow.

In Heaven we will come to know just what a prison our Earthly body had been.

Our loved ones gone before us will be more spiritually advanced than as we knew them on Earth. They may at first look as we remember them, but we will eventually be able to recognize them and know them in their spirit form. The spirit can temporarily change its appearance to accommodate the circumstances.

What counts in Heaven, or Heaven's "test" of a spirit, is one's character. Your material wealth, your station in life, your profession or line of work, your religion...none of those things matter. Your character is who you are and that is what matters. A loving character is one that displays God's goodness and love.

Everything physical is temporary. What is of spirit is eternal.

Material possessions are only temporary. They may not even last a lifetime. They can burn or in some other way be taken from you.

Much concerning the Spirit World is unknown to us and will remain so until we return to it. It is beyond our human comprehension.

As our physical body ages and deteriorates, our spirit can renew and develop as we become more open and receptive to what our spirit guides want us to learn.

There is no need to fear death or fear what comes after death. Our spirit passes over to be joined with our loved ones who have passed before us. It is something to look forward to.

Our spirit lives on as a matter of course after our Earthly life is over. The eternal life of our spirit is not because of any religious belief or church affiliation we have during our life on Earth.

Some spiritualists say that only "spirit guides" who are "high spirits" can help you. I disagree wholeheartedly as I have received several very helpful messages from family members in spirit.

We are here on Earth to learn the truth about our own character. We are to learn how to control and develop ourselves. We can make full use of the things of Earth, but we must learn to be the master of our character and not allow them to master us.

Becoming better evolved while on Earth will speed up one's progression in the Spirit World. Better evolved includes: spiritual awareness and openness to learn, a friendly and compassionate nature, a positive attitude, a ready smile, well behaved, helpful, ability to accept adversaries in a cheerful manner, accepting blame as appropriate and taking responsibility for our actions.

Continued education and refinement in the Spirit World removes one's faults, misbehavior, poor attitude, effects of false teaching experienced on Earth, and any other negatives in order to further develop the spirit toward perfection.

On Earth as we live in the flesh, we are to conduct ourselves in a positive, loving way.

All races, religions, etc. are, as each of us also is, a form of energy created by God. We are all creatures of the same universe and a part of the same Source of energy.

The way we live, how we treat others, and how we respond to God's laws demonstrate how we've developed spiritually, what we believe and value, and whether or not we are in harmony with our Creator.

Being judged by one's works does not necessarily mean what you do for your church and/or give to your church. God knows the heart. The one who never attends church, but lives in harmony with the ways of God is also doing good works. You can't buy your way to a higher spiritual plane. You must prove yourself through enlightenment. Your works must be done for the right reasons. They must be done out of love and compassion for God's creation.

"This, too, shall pass"...the challenges of life are lessons to be learned from for spiritual growth. They are stepping stones to further spiritual enlightenment.

We should live always striving to do the right thing. Be as pure in our heart, mind, and spirit as possible. Show as much love, kindness, and thoughtfulness to others as possible. Smile, laugh, and be pleasant as much as possible.

Our spirit is the energy that makes us who we are. This energy, our spirit, lives on and cannot be destroyed.

The kinder you are to people the more positive interaction you have and the more happy memories you make to later reflect on and smile about.

Wars, feuds, and other unkind acts would be minimized or even non-existent if the example of the life Jesus Christ lived were followed as the standard of religion and as the standard of how we conduct ourselves toward our fellow man.

Any relationship with God is a personal thing between God and the individual. We don't need to follow man-made church doctrines. We should be following the Laws of Nature and the teaching of Jesus Christ. Others should not judge the individual, but instead help their spiritual development through encouragement, not condemnation.

Many Spiritualists may have different names for God, but all believe in the existence of a single supreme power.

There are various levels in the Spirit World that are attained by spiritual growth. Spirits on higher levels teach and develop those on lower levels assisting God in making the "truth" known. Physical life on Earth is a means of learning and developing spiritually to attain a higher level in the Spirit World. You will be judged according to how you chose to live. Did you choose right over wrong? Were you kind and compassionate to your fellow man? Did you seek to learn more about God in order to develop spiritually and become a better person?

Those who have lived on Earth as they should have will attain a higher level than those who did not live right.

A soul makes its own Hell in the Spirit World by holding on to its erroneous convictions and ways. Only after that soul realizes its mistakes will it be free of its self-created Hell.

Hell waits for those who through their ways while incarnate have created it for themselves. Likewise, Heaven waits for those who while incarnate have lived appropriately. The "law of the universe", or God, is love so those who bring pain and suffering upon themselves in their self-created Hell may find happiness by being sorry and remorseful for their ways. They can change for the better and escape their "Hell".

You are the result of your life's thoughts and deeds. You will reap what you have sown. Upon "death" your "sins" are revealed to you. You will see those you've wronged during your incarnate life as well as the result of your "handiwork" on Earth.

The Spirit World is one of positive energy and love.

Earthly material wealth is nothing more than a temporary achievement. You can't take it with you into the Spirit World and it has no value there. How you handle material things while incarnate is what really matters. It is a reflection of your character.

Our consciousness, nature, and experience can lead us to a realization of truth. Those seeking truth evolve by growing in knowledge and wisdom.

Our purpose in our physical life on Earth is to love, be charitable, and to learn and improve through experience, observation, and studying all that we can to better ourselves spiritually and to become more enlightened.

Those in spirit have tremendous love for each of us.

As the physical body prepares to die, pain decreases. The spirit separates from the physical body. Loved ones who have gone on before us will meet us and help us with the transition.

Love is the only true emotion in the Spirit World. We experience negative emotions while incarnate on Earth and hopefully learn to cope with those negative emotions as we progress while incarnate. As we "mellow out" as we age, we are developing spiritually.

You are never alone. There is always at least one member of your spirit family with you.

To meet family we never knew while incarnate and to be reunited with our loved ones who passed on before us is very much something to look forward to.

Free Advice

Get all the advice and instruction you can, so you will be wise the rest of your life. - Proverbs 19:20 (NLT)

Do not worry about Heaven or Hell and where you are headed. You will end up in the Spirit World according to your spiritual development including your heart and deeds while incarnate. You need only worry if you lack love and compassion for your fellow man for in doing so you create your own Hell in the Spirit World where you will remain until you realize your error and work to better yourself.

Understanding the nearness of the two worlds and the possibilities will ease your transition called death.

Live by The Golden Rule, follow the Laws of Nature and the teachings of Jesus. Love others as if each one was you. Don't add grief and/or strife to another's life. If everyone followed these guidelines for living there would be peace and harmony in our world.

We should live always striving to do the right thing. Be as pure in our heart, mind, and spirit as possible. Show as much love, kindness, and thoughtfulness to others as possible. Smile, laugh, and be pleasant as much as possible.

Don't know how to live right? Having trouble treating others right? Keep God's love on your mind and in your heart. Treat others even better than they treat you and if they don't treat you well (or treat you right), don't fall to their level by treating them as they treat you. Realize they still have much yet to learn about love and spiritual matters.

Don't blindly follow anyone, not even a "man of God". Be a free thinker. Study and listen to your intuition and common sense. Is it easier to accept the thinking of someone else than to think for yourself?

Do not fear God, but respect and love God. He created us. He loves us. Respect Him by praying to Him and following His laws and guidance to the best of your ability.

Don't be so busy that you crowd God out of your life. Even just a few minutes each day spent thinking, praying, or meditating will increase your love and understanding of spiritual things.

Can you do more than you are already doing? Pray for wisdom and guidance. Pray for spiritual enlightenment. Trust and have faith.

Our wants and our timing may not be in sync with what's meant to be for us to fulfill our purpose here on Earth. When things don't happen as you would like them to, be patient and understanding. Take a step back and honor what's in the present. This may not be the right time. Your want may not be in your best interest.

The incarnate person consists of body (physical), soul (mind), and spirit (self). Soul and spirit live eternally. Allowing your mind to rule while incarnate is essential to your future happiness. If the body is in control, you will have unhappiness and much more to answer for after the incarnate life ends.

View life events – good or bad – as important steps to aligning you with your purpose for being here on Earth. Look at events in your life, especially difficult and negative ones from a positive perspective. See them as lessons learned for spiritual development. Look for the positive aspects of bad experiences and mistakes made in order to see how they've made you grow, prepare, and become who you now are...a better person.

Mistakes are only mistakes if you haven't learned from them. Each one is an opportunity to learn and improve one's self.

You can't go back and undo what you regret having said or done, but you can apologize and try to make amends. If you feel you have wronged someone who has passed away, send thoughts their way. They will receive them and understand.

When reading about Spiritualism, please don't be disheartened, confused, or overwhelmed by the various explanations of the Spirit World and life after the death of the body. There are conflicting accounts of how many levels the Spirit World consists of, how many Earth incarnations are required to develop spiritually, the purpose of the other planets in the universe, the definition of God and Jesus, and many other details. These things do not matter very much to me. What matters to me is whether or not I'm learning what I'm here to learn, whether or not I'm developing into a better person thereby developing further spiritually, and whether or not I'm striving to be the best person I can be and continuing to "do well" as my older brother in a message said I was doing at that time. Forget the conflicting accounts. Some of it is very likely true while some of it may come from a more creative imagination than you or I have. Each author claims to have received the knowledge they have shared through some type of communication with a spirit who is either known to them, was previously unknown to them, or who is their own "higher power" who they have temporarily separated from to experience their current incarnation on Earth.

If you're confused as to what to believe, don't be. Pray for guidance and wisdom then leave it up to the words and leading of God not man. If man says you're living wrong, don't take it to heart. Man is not to judge, that is for God to do. God knows your heart and if you're truly doing what you feel is right and seeking God's will for your life you're doing fine.

To grow spiritually and become God-like, one must practice faith, love, and charity. One must break from ego manifestations and power struggles as these will cause disharmony and despair leading to inner unhappiness. The sooner one keeps ego in check and breaks from any power struggle and self-centeredness the better and the sooner one can grow spiritually altering one's character in a very positive manner.

The foremost need of one's soul is time to think.

It is your attitude that makes you who you are: sinner, saint, or something between. A change in attitude will change that life.

Share wisdom by setting an example. What is said by example can speak louder and be more important than words.

If your life has been difficult, try not to be disheartened. You've experienced what has come your way in life to learn, grow spiritually, and become a better person. All you've been through has placed you closer to a higher plane in Heaven if such planes exist. A lifetime on Earth is so short in duration when compared to the eternity you've improved for yourself by your experiences and lessons learned here.

Before writing off Spiritualism and communication with the Spirit World, attend a Spiritualist church, receive a few messages (just one message might convince you as it did me), and then form your opinion. If you think it's all "of the Devil", please remember that Jesus Himself talked with Satan and allowed Himself to be tempted by Satan. Spiritualism, as is found in the many churches I've attended, is not demonic. It is Godly. It is reverent. It is love. It is enlightenment.

The words spoken by Jesus in His "Sermon on the Mount", as found in *The Holy Bible*, book of Matthew, chapters five through seven, if followed and adhered to, are all that's needed to live a life that is acceptable to God.

Though we may stumble at times due to our human nature and imperfection we can still get up and continue to strive to live a Godly life. Gradually we will become more enlightened and achieve greater spiritual growth.

We should seek God's guidance, honestly examine ourselves and allow Him to guide us, and then give Him thanks for the help He has given.

A prayer at the start of each day inviting God to be with you, a sense of continued fellowship with God throughout the day, and then a prayer of thanks at the end of the day is a good plan to grow spiritually.

Don't worry about seeing and doing everything there is to do in this world during your incarnate lifetime. You'll still have opportunities when in spirit. (My uncle in spirit said he can attend any sporting event he wants to!)

Don't expect to receive complete enlightenment while incarnate. Few people, if any, have sufficient time available to dedicate to the prayer and meditation necessary to receive all there is. But, we can strive to learn as much as our schedule allows for what we're able to learn now will help us progress in the Spirit World. Limit the amount of time you spend watching or participating in humor that belittles others and try to find joy for yourself in more positive ways. Gradually you will see more of the God-created beauty in things and won't seek gratification at the expense of others.

There are various ways to find answers to your questions about faith, religion, Christianity, Spiritualism, etc. I recommend you get several opinions from various sources including the Internet, friends, family, ministers, and books. After gathering those different viewpoints, consider the source and possible bias of each one, pray for wisdom and guidance, consider the various possibilities, and draw your own conclusion based on what seems right and logical to you.

Don't become so wrapped up in serving a church that you neglect serving God. If your church teaches hatred toward other religions or denominations, it is not teaching God's love. Don't become so dependent upon a church or church leader such as a pastor that you no longer depend upon God and cease praying to Him for wisdom and guidance. Your pastor is not God. Your church is not God. If your church's doctrine and the pastor's sermons conflict with your personal beliefs and convictions, research the source of your belief and compare it to the church's or pastor's source. If yours still holds firm, you may be better off finding a like-minded group with whom to worship. Don't allow the doctrine and dogmas of any church or the opinions of other Christians to make you feel any less of a Christian if you are truly living as you believe you should. If you are comfortable in your beliefs, and know you're right with God, you're doing well and are on the right track. Don't be derailed by any church or judgmental individual if your heart is right.

To close my "Free Advice" chapter, I'd like to share with you a poem from the back of the "Order of Service" bulletin I received from the Christian Spiritualist Temple in Columbus, Ohio. There is no mention of an author.

Seed Thoughts

The mind is a garden where thought flowers grow.

The thoughts that we think are the seeds that we sow.

Each kind loving thought bears a kind loving deed

While a thought that is selfish is just like a weed.

We must watch what we think the livelong day,

Pull out the weed thoughts and throw them away,

Plant loving seed thoughts so thick in a row

There will be no room for weed thoughts to grow.

Epilogue

Unfortunately, a lot of negativity has come to be associated with Spiritualism because of the position of most Christian churches against it and the failure of the majority of people to openly and honestly educate themselves instead of depending on the view of the church and others who haven't done so. They believe Spiritualism consists of fortunetellers and other "psychics" who are frauds and prey upon those who long to communicate with a passed loved one or wish to know what the future holds for them.

I myself visited a couple of these fortuneteller/psychics in my younger years and it seems there's always a costly "catch" you must purchase from them before your life will be happy. One told me I needed to pay her one hundred dollars for the purchase of two candles she would burn as she prayed for me in order to drive the evil and negative influences out of my life so that I could find happiness and success. The other psychic wanted one hundred dollars to interpret the many dreams I would be having that would guide me through life and help me to make the right choices. These frauds are not what I've found in the Spiritualist churches. It's no wonder that with frauds like these along with the negative teaching of most Christian churches condemning Spiritualism, so many people believe it to be a demonic thing.

But, those misled people haven't experienced what I have experienced. Some are so convinced it's either wrong or it's impossible to communicate with spirits that they absolutely refuse to discuss, see, hear, or read anything about it. They are like my close friend who has no desire to hear about my experiences at Spiritualist churches and told me anyone who thinks they can talk to dead people is crazy. He's of course entitled to his opinion, but I'm reasonably certain that I'm not crazy and I believe he's in for a rude awakening (and a wonderful surprise) when he passes over.

Spiritualism is not demonic. It's not the working of any anti-Christ force. The teachings of Jesus Christ are also those of Spiritualism. Jesus taught love, compassion, generosity, and service to our fellow man. He taught us *"love thy neighbor as thyself"* (Mark 12:31 KJV), *"as ye would that men should do to you, do ye also to them likewise"* (Luke 6:31 KJV), and so on. Spiritualism also teaches these doctrines. The same laws that Jesus taught his disciples by which to live and carry out their work are the same laws taught by Spiritualism.

The twelve disciples of Jesus included one who betrayed Him and another who three times denied Him, but that doesn't make Christianity a bad thing. I have written in this book about pastors and other church leaders who were spiritually weak or uncaring or in some other way a poor example of a "man of God". A few bad examples do not make all of Christianity bad. So likewise it is with Spiritualism. There have been some who have been proven to be frauds and were only in it to make money through deception, but that doesn't make true Spiritualism something fraudulent or evil.

The Spiritualist churches I've attended and the mediums with whom I have had contact are loving, caring individuals who want nothing more than to help others see that we have a Divine Creator who loves us and that there is a wonderful continuing life awaiting us in the Spirit World filled with beauty, love, and further enlightenment for our spiritual development.

Perhaps Spiritualism is one of the mysteries that Jesus spoke of when His disciples asked why He spoke in parables. In Luke 8:10 (KJV) we read, *And he said, Unto you it is given to know the mysteries of the kingdom of God: but to others in parables; that seeing they might not see, and hearing they might not understand.* Paul speaks several times in his writings about Jesus being a mystery revealed by God to His people. Spiritualism may be another mystery that God has revealed to us.

Job said, according to Job 12:22 (KJV), *"He discovereth deep things out of darkness, and bringeth out to light the shadow of death."* The "He" Job is talking about here is God. God has brought out to light the shadow of death through Spiritualism.

Could it be that God first gave us His Son, Jesus Christ, who Christians consider to be the Way to eternal life, and now that our spiritual enlightenment has advanced beyond that of the people centuries ago, God has given us Spiritualism to offer us proof that eternal life does exist beyond the life we are now living?

I can't prove to you that my experiences involving messages from passed loved ones actually happened. You only have my word that the messages I received had true meaning to me and were received through mediums that had never before met or ever heard of me. The best advice I could give someone who is interested in experiencing what I have, that is communicating with those in spirit, is to attend a Spiritualist church at least until such time that you receive a message.

Depending upon the size of the church congregation, the amount of time allowed, and the number of mediums available, you may not get a message every service you attend. I attended four or five services before receiving my first message.

Now, because there are no Spiritualist Churches closer than a seven-hour drive from my home, when I do get the rare chance to attend, I always get a message from one of my parents and often from more than one family member. It seems they're as anxious to communicate with me as I am to hear from them.

The death of our physical body is not something we should fear, but rather an event for us to look forward to, for what awaits us in the "afterlife" is love beyond our comprehension and beauty beyond our imagination. We will be reunited with our loved ones who have already passed, we can be with our loved ones who are still incarnate, and through Spiritualist mediums we can even give them messages of help and encouragement as I have received on many occasions.

Information About Spiritualism

The following information may be very useful to the reader interested in knowing more about Spiritualism. I know of two main groups of Modern Spiritualists, the Spiritualists and the Christian Spiritualists. I have attended churches of both groups and have felt very comfortable in all of the Spiritualist churches I've attended. (As I mentioned earlier, most of the Spiritualist churches I've attended have been in England. Spiritualism is much more widespread in England than it is in America. The city I visit in England has three Spiritualist churches.)

My personal beliefs may align better with the Christian Spiritualists because of my Christian upbringing, but since mankind has many names for our Divine Creator, it doesn't bother me to hear God called by a name other than the one I'm used to calling Him.

To show some of the difference between the two Spiritualist groups, I will share with you the *Declaration of Principles* for each group. The principles of the two groups are basically the same, just worded differently.

Those of the Christian Spiritualists are from an "Order of Service" I received when I attended the Christian Spiritualist Temple in Columbus, Ohio. Their website found at http://www.christianspiritualisttemple.org includes plenty of additional information including links to other sites of interest. It's well worth visiting.

Declaration of Principles (Christian Spiritualist)

> We believe in God.
>
> Physical and Spiritual Nature are the expression of God's creation.
>
> A correct understanding of Nature and living in the spirit of God constitute true religion.
>
> The existence and personal identity of the individual continue after the change we call death.
>
> Communication with the so-called dead is a fact proven by the existence of Spiritualism.
>
> The highest morality is contained in the golden rule: "Do unto others as you would have them do unto you."
>
> Each person is responsible for their own happiness or unhappiness as they obey or disobey natural, physical, and spiritual laws.
>
> The doorway to reformation is never closed against any human soul, here or hereafter.
>
> The precept of prophecy contained in the Bible is a divine attribute proven through mediumship.

The *Declaration of Principles* of the Spiritualists and the information following through to the end of the questions and answers are taken from the National Spiritualist Association of Churches' *NSAC Spiritualist Manual, 20th Edition* as well as from their website found at http://www.nsac.org.[1]

I highly recommend their manual and website as both provide much more information about Spiritualism than what I've included here.

Declaration of Principles (Spiritualist Church – specifically National Spiritualist Association of Churches)

1. We believe in Infinite Intelligence.

2. We believe that the phenomena of nature, both physical and spiritual, are the expression of Infinite Intelligence.

3. We affirm that a correct understanding of such expression and living in accordance therewith constitute true religion.

4. We affirm that the existence and personal identity of the individual continue after the change called death.

5. We affirm that communication with the so-called dead is a fact, scientifically proven by the phenomena of Spiritualism.

---

[1] Reprinted with permission from The NSAC Spiritualist Manual, 20th Edition, published October 2017, by National Spiritualist Association of Churches, and from their website, www.nsac.org.

6. We believe that the highest morality is contained in the Golden Rule: *Do unto others as you would have them do unto you.*

7. We affirm the moral responsibility of individuals and that we make our own happiness or unhappiness as we obey or disobey Nature's physical and spiritual laws.

8. We affirm that the doorway to reformation is never closed against any soul here or hereafter.

9. We affirm that the precepts of Prophecy and Healing are divine attributes proven through Mediumship.

Simplified Form:

1. We believe in God.

2. We believe that God is expressed through all Nature.

3. True religion is living in obedience to Nature's Laws.

4. We never die.

5. Spiritualism proves that we can talk with people in the Spirit World.

6. Be kind, do good, and others will do likewise.

7. We bring unhappiness to ourselves by the errors we make and we will be happy if we obey the laws of life.

8. Every day is a new beginning.

9. Prophecy and healing are expressions of God.

Interpretation:

By Joseph P. Whitwell, Third NSAC President, 1925-1944

1. By this we express our belief in a supreme Impersonal Power, everywhere present, manifesting as life, through all forms of organized matter, called by some, God; by others, Spirit; and by Spiritualists, Infinite Intelligence. Though this power is impersonal, our understanding can only be gained by our personal perception of this creative force.

2. In this manner we express our belief in the immanence of Spirit and that all forms of life are manifestations of Spirit or Infinite Intelligence, and thus, all men [people] are children of God.

3. A correct understanding of the Laws of Nature on the physical, mental, and spiritual planes of life and living in accordance therewith will unfold the highest aspirations and attributes of the soul, which is the correct function of true Religion.

4. *Life here and hereafter is all one life whose continuity of consciousness is unbroken by that mere change in form whose process we call death.* (Lilian Whiting)

5. Spirit communication has been in evidence in all ages of the world and is amply recorded in both sacred and profane literature of all ages. Orthodoxy has accepted these manifestations and has interpreted them in dogma and creed in terms of the supernatural. Spiritualism accepts and recognizes these manifestations and interprets them in the understanding and light of Natural Law.

6. This precept (*principle*) we believe to be true. It points the way to harmony, peace, and happiness. Wherever tried, it has proven successful, and when fully understood and practiced, it will bring peace and happiness to all of humanity.

7. Individuals are responsible for the welfare of the world in which they live; for its welfare or its misery, for its happiness or unhappiness, and if we are to obtain heaven upon earth, we must learn to make that heaven, for ourselves and for others. Individuals are responsible for their own spiritual growth and welfare. Errors and wrongdoing must be outgrown and overcome. Virtue and love of good must take their place. Spiritual growth and advancement must be attained by aspiration and personal striving. Vicarious atonement has no place in the philosophy of Spiritualism. Individuals must bear their own burdens in overcoming wrongdoings and replace them with right actions.

8. We discard entirely the terrible wrong and illogical teaching of eternal damnation, and in place thereof, we accept and present for consideration of thinking people the thought of the continuity of life beyond the change called death.

[This is} A natural life, where the opportunities for growth and progress to better, higher, and more spiritual conditions are open to all, even as they are here on the earth plane of life. We accept no such teaching as a *hell fire*, but we do teach that transgression of Natural Law and wrongdoing will necessarily bring remorse and suffering that would be difficult to describe in words and which can only be relieved by the individual's own efforts, if not here, then in the hereafter. If we make our own lives better while here, and that of our neighbors happier, we shall unfold that happiness or heaven on earth, which we shall carry with us into the Spirit World.

9. We thus affirm our belief in and acceptance of the truths that Prophecy, Mediumship, and Healing are not unique, but are universal, everlasting, and have been witnessed and observed in all ages.

History:

Principles 1-6 adopted in Chicago, Illinois, 1899

Principles 7-8 adopted in Rochester, New York, 1909

Principle 9 adopted in St. Louis, Missouri, 1944

Principle 9 revised in Oklahoma City, 1983

Principle 9 revised in Westfield, New Jersey, 1998

Principle 8 revised in Rochester, New York, 2001

Principle 6 revised in Ronkonkoma, New York, 2004

Defining Spiritualism

Adopted by the National Spiritualist Association of Churches

Spiritualism is the Science, Philosophy, and Religion of continuous life, based upon the demonstrated fact of communication, by means of mediumship, with those who live in the Spirit World. (1919)

Spiritualism Is a Science because it investigates, analyzes and classifies facts and manifestations demonstrated from the spirit side of life.

Spiritualism Is a Philosophy because it studies the Laws of Nature both on the seen and unseen sides of life and bases its conclusions upon present observed facts. It accepts statements of observed facts of past ages and conclusions drawn therefrom, when sustained by reason and by results of observed facts of the present day.

Spiritualism Is a Religion because it strives to understand and to comply with the Physical, Mental and Spiritual Laws of Nature, which are the laws of God.

Information About Spiritualism

A **Spiritualist** is one who believes, as the basis of his or her religion, in the communication between this and the Spirit World by means of mediumship and who endeavors to mold his or her character and conduct in accordance with the highest teachings derived from such communication. (1914, Rev. 1938)

A **Medium** is one whose organism is sensitive to vibrations from the spirit world and through whose instrumentality, intelligences in that world are able to convey messages and produce the phenomena of Spiritualism. (1914)

A **Spiritualist Healer** is one who, either through one's own inherent powers or through mediumship, is able to impart vital, curative force to pathologic conditions. (1930, 1993)

The **Phenomena of Spiritualism** consists of both mental and physical demonstrations of mediumship. Among these are Apports, Automatic and Independent Writings and Paintings, Clairalience, Clairaudience, Clairsentience, Clairvoyance, Gift of Tongues, Healing or Laying-on-of-Hands, Levitation, Materialization, Precipitation, Prophecy, Psychometry, Raps, Spirit Photography, Trance, Transfiguration, Trumpet *(Independent Voice)*, Visions, Voice. These and any other manifestations proving the continuity of life, as demonstrated through the physical and spiritual senses and faculties of humanity, are commonly known as mediumship.

Religion

Spiritualism is a common sense religion, one of knowing and living. We accept all truths and endeavor to prove their validity. Truths are found in nature, in other religions, in writings, in science, in philosophy, in Divine Law and are received through spirit communication.

Spiritualists believe that God or Infinite Intelligence is ALL That Is, expressing through all creation by love, light, and law. Humanity, the most complex of life on earth, reaches this Divine Source through prayer, meditation, listening to the inner awareness, and service. Why service? Because every living thing is a part of God, so as we serve life we also serve the Higher Energies.

Life is consciousness – without consciousness there is no existence. Consciousness is the totality of one's thoughts, feelings, emotions, and impressions on the mind. The state of thinking is how we create our consciousness. Spiritualism teaches that through the Law of Action/Reaction or Cause/Effect we take control of our lives as we control our thoughts. Positive thinking leads to happiness and assists the individual to grow.

Spiritualism encourages growth of loving consciousness in the physical world not only for the immediate benefits, but also the future rewards in the Spiritual Dimension. The Law of Continuity and the Law of Attraction teach us that "As within, so without. As above, so below." A soul arriving in the next plane of existence will find they take their consciousness with them and will be in the company of like-minded entities. The more loving and spiritual the soul has become, the more beautiful and rewarding will be the new home and associates in the spirit land.

Life is continuous, the consciousness never dies for it is part of God and the Infinite is forever. Upon the cessation of the physical housing the spirit graduates to the next plane of existence. This plane is similar to our earthly plane but at a higher rate of vibration and luminosity. One method of service in spirit is to communicate, assist and help illuminate those that are living on the earth plane. Mediums in the Spirit World and mediums in the physical world adjust their vibrations to enable communications between the two planes of existence. It has been demonstrated in our Churches, home circles and in scientific investigations that "there is no death, there are no dead."

All life moves in a gradual state of evolution or change. Arrival in the Spiritual realm does not mean instant knowing. Rather the personality of the individual and the understanding gleaned on the earth plane continue at the same level, ready to begin the next phase of unfoldment. The physical world has aches, pains and struggles. These are not taken to the spiritual realm which is love, light, law, peace, cooperation, sharing, and growth. The soul body is whole and shining forth that which is within its essence. Falsehoods, separateness, and illusions are left behind as the desire to progress awakens. The rewards follow according to the goodness of the entity.

Life concerns growth. We, Spiritualists, try to keep an open, even mind so new truths may be incorporated into our principles. In keeping with this, we have no bound creed or set of dogmas. Our Declaration of Principles, which form the basis of our beliefs, has changed over the years as new clarification has been gleaned. We know that truth is the highest religion and endeavor to test our beliefs, altering them as new truths are proven.

Humans are spiritual beings, an indivisible part of the Divine. God is The Spirit within each individual waiting to be consciously accepted and activated. One of the desires of Spiritualism is to awaken this spirit within, to move beyond the five senses to higher awareness. Each person has free choice and is personally responsible, yet Spiritualism, through communication with the higher teachings derived from the Spirit World, tries to provide a way, a guideline, a set of principles, to help the world travelers to proceed upward, toward the light. The following pages briefly present the message of Spiritualism.

Ancient and Modern Spiritualism

So often in a lecture or a book, we hear the term "Modern American Spiritualism". Why Modern? It is Modern Spiritualism to distinguish it from the ancient form of Spiritualism, for spiritual manifestations and communications between the physical world and the spiritual world have been evident and recorded by all civilizations. In fact, every religion that has ever been, has registered Spirit manifestations. Most all of the great spiritual leaders conversed or communicated with spirits although they were called other names, such as devas, pitris, gods, ancestral spirits, ghosts, and magic.

Often, in the beginning of recorded history, people believed in many gods. There was a god that dwelled in all of nature's manifestations, such as a sun god, a god of wind and storms, a god of earth, etc. If some problem arose, the individual or group felt that they had in some way displeased the gods. Sometimes offerings or sacrifices were made to appease the gods. Those in the past believed in many gods that were apart from them, where we in Spiritualism believe in one God, that we call Infinite Intelligence, which is All in All or within everything.

The people were uneducated as a whole so much that happened must have been rather frightening, or seemed like miracles or magic.

We, in Modern Spiritualism, know that all flows according to Natural Law. Where the ancients believed in the supernatural, miracles and magic, punishment and rewards, we believe in the natural, God's Laws, growth and love. We are a truth-seeking religion that incorporates science and testing as a part of our philosophy.

Often the people of the past thought of phenomena as the work of devils and demons. Some religions today still see communication in this manner. We know that the phenomena is a work through those in the Spirit World and that we attract to us spirit guides that correspond to the level of our vibration.

Ancient (625 BC to 476 AD) humanity thought objectively. They made their reflections upon life by looking at the universe as a whole, then attempting to see the interconnections between things. The early thinkers looked at the differences between things, the realities and non-realities, then tried to figure out how the world was constructed based upon this point of view of the world.

Medieval Philosophy (476 AD – 1453 AD) is considered traditional in their thinking which means that they had a set of authoritative doctrines from the past. During the Middle Ages, it is said that humanity, no matter how deeply they reflected, was constrained by a set of religious traditions and censors.

Modern thought is subjective. Here we refer to an entire change in the type of intellect where the starting point is not considered the world, but the individual. We now see that truths can be found within rather than externally. Reality is personal rather than the cosmos of the ancients of the political state of the middle period.

Modern American Spiritualism began on March 31, 1848, with the Fox family establishing communication with the departed murdered spirit of Charles B. Rosna. Much of the basic philosophy that we have tested was given to our pioneers through spirit communication. While Spiritualism began in America, it has spread over the entire world. Thus, to make a short phase long, this is why we call our religion, MODERN AMERICAN SPIRITUALISM.

Quotes from Dr. Victoria Barnes, M.D.

Spiritualism is a provable religion of naturalness based upon physical and spiritual manifestations of the great universal, immutable, eternal Natural Law governing both finite and infinite expressions found in the mortal and immortal worlds.

It reveals the nature of humanity, the nature of the universe in which we live, and our inter-relatedness to each other. It stresses the unfoldment of the soul's potentialities mediumship as the avenue through which our knowledge of an after-life has come, also proof that regardless of what stage of existence we are in, such is but a fractional part of our eternal existence for it is all ONE LIFE.

Through mediumship, communication with mortals who have experienced transition from earth has been established, thus proving, THERE IS NO DEATH

We are all souls now, each clothed in a material body through which our mental and spiritual faculties function. Within this material body is the spiritual or etheric body which serves as the vehicle for soul expression the moment transition occurs...

At transition, we enter a world of entirely different environment and purpose where we have no more use for the material body that has been shed and laid away, than we have for the overcoat in summer. The spiritual body is suited to the conditions of the Spirit World; it is this body that is used for spirit-return.

Spirit-return, according to our present knowledge, is governed by three contributing factors:

LOVE for those still on Earth, DESIRE to prove they still live; and PURPOSE, as contained in the requirements for understanding the operations of Natural Law governing all expressions in the universe, and the inter-relatedness of the material and spiritual worlds......

If Spirit could not return, then the incidents recorded in all the Bibles of the world are falsehoods, and the religions built upon and around these occurrences have been built upon the sands. But, these religions have endured which would indicate their foundations had been more secure than sand. Our present mediums are proving spirit return has never ceased.

Quotations

Confucianism	What you don't want done to yourself, don't do to others.
Buddhism	Hurt not others with that which pains thyself
Jainism	In happiness and suffering, in joy and grief, we should regard all creatures as we regard our own self, and should therefore refrain from inflicting upon others such injury as would appear

	undesirable to us if inflicted upon ourselves.
Zoroastrianism	Do not unto others all that which is not well for oneself.
Classical Paganism	May I do to others as I would that they should do unto me.
Hinduism	Do naught to others which if done to thee would cause thee pain.
Judaism	What is hateful to yourself, don't do to your fellow man.
Christianity	Whatsoever ye would that men should do to you, do ye even so to them.
Sikhism	Treat others as thou wouldst be treated thyself.

The Philosophy of Spiritualism

The following Declaration of Principles is published to the world, not as a creed binding on the conscious of the individual, but as the consensus of a very large majority of Spiritualists on the fundamental teachings of Spiritualism:

We believe in Infinite Intelligence.

We believe that the phenomena of Nature, both physical and spiritual, are the expression of Infinite Intelligence.

We affirm that a correct understanding of such expression and living in accordance therewith, constitute true religion.

We affirm that the existence and personal identity of the individual continue after the change called death.

We affirm that communication with the so-called dead is a fact, scientifically proven by the phenomena of Spiritualism.

We believe that the highest morality is contained in the Golden Rule: "Do unto others as you would have them do unto you."

We affirm the moral responsibility of individuals, and that we make our own happiness or unhappiness as we obey or disobey Nature's physical and spiritual laws.

We affirm that the doorway to reformation is never closed against any human soul here or hereafter.

We affirm that the precepts of Prophecy and Healing are Divine attributes proven through Mediumship.

Natural Law

Spiritualists, through contact that is made with those that have passed to the other side of life, affirm the interrelatedness of all life. One clue that a person is beginning to become further intuned and more cosmic, is when the egoistic, self-serving portion of the individual diminishes and the universal consciousness comes to the forefront. Prominent in this consciousness is the awareness of the Universal Laws.

The religion of Spiritualism encourages all humankind to learn and practice living in accordance with God's Laws. What are these Universal Laws? How many of them are there and do they apply to everyone? Infinite Intelligence is Love, Light and Law. Though many use a certain number of laws as guidelines, there is no set number of laws. Just as Love and Light are not limited, so the Law is not limited, as Infinite Intelligence is not limited. Neither does the Law limit those who strive to follow it. Rather, it sets them free and shows them the way to grow, live in peace and be happy.

The study of Natural Law is very beneficial to all. A few brief points to consider are that the laws are just, impartial, consistent, non-judgmental, automatic, immutable, impersonal, affects the physical, mental and spiritual, is unchangeable and the underlying control of the universe, ensuring progressive evolution. Natural Law is the connecting link, providing constant order to the universe. It governs the visible and invisible, the animate and inanimate in the mortal and immortal worlds.

Natural Law is like a kind teacher that understands we learn by doing. The law gently points out our mistakes that we may grow and use the insight to our benefit. The law uses the reflecting ethers as a mirror to show us the way. It verifies personal responsibility and individualization.

All things in life interrelate and so it is with the laws. They are evident in mathematics, geometry, mechanics, plant life, seasons, etc. We can use the laws to choose love, light, peace, growth and joy. The universe is propelled by law and impelled by love.

Just a few laws to demonstrate the totality of the Laws:

The Law of Desire

The Law of Harmony

The Law of Mind

The Law of Cause and Effect

The Law of Vibration

The Law of Passivity

The Law of Supply and Demand

The Law of Love

The Law of Life/Light

The Law of Thought

The Law of Compensation/Retribution

The Law of Adhesion/Cohesion

The Law of Evolution

The Law of Continuity

The Law of Attraction/Affinity

The Golden Rule

The Law of Cooperation

The Law of Balance/Polarity

The Law of Cycles/Periodicity

The Law of Gravitation

The Law of Productivity/Receptivity

As the seeker strives to understand Natural Law, they are presented with the truths of the universe. God's Law is immutable and we know of no instances that it has been set aside, therefore, there are no miracles for all is in accordance with the operation of the Spiritual Laws. Infinite Intelligence has given us these constructive, progressive patterns to guide our existence now and forever more. The God of the Universe impregnates the spirit of all, then lets it alone to discover itself through light, love and law. As we learn more of these laws, we learn more of Infinite Intelligence. Emerson wrote, "The finite alone has wrought and suffered, the Infinite lies stretched in smiling repose." The Infinite Spirit within us shows us the way to shine.

Spiritual Mediumship

A medium is one whose organism is sensitive to vibrations from the Spirit World and through whose instrumentality, intelligences in that world are able to convey messages and produce the phenomena of Spiritualism. The phenomena of Spiritualism consists of:

prophecy, clairvoyance, clairaudience, gift of tongues, laying on of hands, healing, visions, trance, apports, revelations, raps, levitation, automatic and independent writing and painting, photography, materialization, psychometry, direct and independent voice, and any other manifestation which proves the continuity of life.

"The office of mediumship is to bless humanity, to enable the race to overcome conditions of matter sufficiently to make such the servant rather than the master of intelligent beings, to enable it to guide (through intuition) the individual for their own and others good." Mary T. Longley from "Teachings and Illustrations As They Emanate From The Spirit World."

Spiritual Healing

Spiritual healing, recognized in many ancient religions, has been a principle of Spiritualism since its beginning. Today, on a national basis, evidence is growing in the medical community of the importance of spiritual healing to the cure of the individual in need. Evidence is growing that the whole person needs treatment, not just the illness.

A Spiritualist Healer is one who, either through his or her own inborn power or through mediumship, is able to transmit curative energies to physical conditions. The results of Spiritual Healing are produced in several ways:

By spiritual influences working through the body of the medium to transmit curative energies to the diseased parts of the recipient's body.

By spiritual influences enlightening the mind of the medium so that the cause, nature, and seat of the disease in the recipient is made known to the medium.

Through the application of absent healing treatments whereby spiritual beings combine their own healing energies with the energies of the medium and cause them to be absorbed by the system of the recipient.

A Spiritualist Healer works with the spirit, mind, emotions, and the body of the recipient. A Spiritualist Healer is aware that once stress is removed from the mind and emotions, the body will respond naturally. This brings about holistic healing in the patient.

Spiritualist Healers acknowledge the importance of the medical community and work in cooperation with it at all times. Spiritualism recognizes that the medical community is an instrument of healing of the Infinite.

Prayer for Spiritual Healing

I ask the great unseen healing force

to remove all obstructions from my mind and body

and to restore me to perfect health.

I ask this in all sincerity and honesty

and I will do my part.

I ask this great unseen healing force

to help both present and absent ones

who are in need of help

and to restore them to perfect health.

I put my trust in the love and power of God.

The Objects of Spiritualism

The object *(goal, intention, motive)* of the organized movement of Spiritualism as represented by the National Spiritualist Association of Churches may be stated in part as follows:

> To teach the truths and principles expressed in the Declaration of Principles and in the definition of Spiritualism, a Spiritualist, a Medium, and a Spiritualist Healer.
>
> To teach and proclaim the Science, Philosophy and Religion of Modern Spiritualism;
>
> To encourage lectures on all subjects pertaining to the spiritual and secular welfare of humanity;
>
> To protest against every attempt to compel humanity to worship God in any particular or prescribed manner;
>
> To advocate and promote spiritual healing.
>
> To protect and encourage spiritual teachers and mediums in all laudable efforts in giving evidence of proof to humanity of a continued intercourse [communication] and relationship between the living and the so-called dead [those who have made their transition to the Spirit World].

> To encourage every person in holding present beliefs always open to restatement as growing thought and investigation reveal understanding of new truths thereby leaving every individual free to follow the dictates of reason and conscience in spiritual as in secular affairs.

Following are a few questions and answers taken from the NSAC website which the reader may find helpful:

> Q. Why is Spiritualism Important Today, More Than Ever?
>
> A. Spiritualists come from every walk of life. We are bankers, builders, nurses, teachers, bookkeepers, sales clerks, electricians – any and all professions are attracted to Spiritualism. Every place you find thinking men and women coming together, you will find Spiritualists. Spiritualism is a science, philosophy and religion that satisfies your logic, your mind and your heart. As the population contemplates the current conditions in the world today, they are seeking a greater understanding of the purpose of life and what can be done to improve individual life situations and the circumstances of the world. Spiritualism gives a person the key that can be used to find the answers she/he seeks. Spiritualism provides the knowledge that by using prayer and meditation, we can become more aware of our responsibilities to ourselves and to others. Through this inner awareness and guidance

received through spirit communications, a person takes the necessary actions to improve his or her own life and contributes to the improved welfare of the entire human race.

Spiritualism is the KEY that sets humanity free! Free to live and grow in the physical through love and law; and free because we know that life is continuous, the spirit never dies. "There is no death, there are no dead."

Q. What Is a Spiritualist?

A. A Spiritualist is one who believes, as the basis of his or her religion, in the communication between this and the spirit world by means of mediumship, and who endeavors to mold his or her character and conduct in accordance with the highest teachings derived from such communication.

Q. Can a Spiritualist Accept the Teaching of Jesus?

A. Yes. A belief in spirit communication does not conflict with the Teachings ascribed to Jesus. The Christian Bible confirms its truth repeatedly. However, Spiritualism is not a branch of Christianity or other major religion. Spiritualism has been recognized by the US Congress as a separate and distinct religion.

Q. Is Spiritualism a Religion?

A. It is a Religion, Philosophy, and Science in one. It has a national organization, state associations, numbers of churches, and a solemnly ordained ministry.

Q. What Should Convince Me of Its Truths?

A. Your own reason and common sense after a thorough and scientific investigation.

Many more questions are answered by the National Spiritualist Association of Churches in their manual and on their website.[2] The website also includes a directory of Spiritualist churches.

Please be aware, should you choose to do an Internet search for "Spiritualist Churches", some of the churches displayed in your search may not practice Spiritualism. Some may be churches that teach a way to live a more spiritual life, but do not practice communication with the Spirit World. One search I did brought up a church called "Spiritual Life Center" and another called "Spiritual Living Church". When I checked further on the websites, I found these two to be churches teaching spirituality, but not Spiritualism. Each church website usually contains a page explaining their beliefs. Please check the beliefs of the church before attending a service there with the hope of experiencing spirit messages or clairvoyance.

You may also find "Metaphysical" churches that believe in proof of continued life through communication with the Spirit World, but do not use the word "Spiritualist" in the title of the church. One such church I've attended is The First United Metaphysical Chapel in Bahama, North Carolina. Their website,

---

[2] Referring here to The NSAC Spiritualist Manual, 20th Edition, published October 2017, by National Spiritualist Association of Churches and to their website, www.nsac.org.

http://tfumc.net/, contains information about the church and their beliefs plus a video about Spiritualism and audio recordings of their sermons.

A couple of other interesting bits about Spiritualism:

The symbol of Spiritualism is the sunflower.

The motto of Spiritualism:

> As the sunflower turns its face toward the light of the sun, so Spiritualism turns the face of humanity toward the light of truth.

Spiritualism's greatest value lies in the fact that, when its truth is generally accepted, it will completely revolutionize many accepted but antiquated ideas and customs. In what way could that be possible? Because Spiritualism proves not only that we continue to exist consciously after the death of the physical body, but that we are then still responsible for our actions while here. We cannot escape the consequences of our acts, good or bad. Therefore, if a majority of earth's inhabitants become firmly convinced of this fact, plainly the glaring defects and abuses of our present life will gradually disappear, as each individual will exercise greater care not to injure others, because of the consequences and resultant injuries to self. – Author Unknown

About the Author

(In case you're interested)

As I complete this book, I am a 64-year-old man blessed by my Creator with life, good physical health, and a loving family. I was raised by two parents who took good care of their children and raised them as well as they knew how to do and, in my opinion, my parents did a fine job. Unfortunately for parents (myself included), children don't come with any "how to" manual. I know my siblings and I caused more than a few trying times for our parents. Fortunately for me, my children have been much less trying than I was. I've been blessed in this life with four awesome children, one wonderful daughter-in-law, and two lovely grandchildren.

I was born and raised in Long Beach, California, a great place in which to grow up at the time. I moved from that area at age 36 and spent the next 17 years near Sacramento, California, in an area with thousands more peaches and prunes than people. In 2006, I transferred within the company I worked for at that time and moved to a humid and hurricane-prone area near Houston, Texas, to have my children closer together. It was nice to be back by the ocean. Hurricane Ike paid us a memorable visit after I'd been there for two years. After nine years in Texas, and after being forced into an early retirement, I moved to northeast Alabama away from big cities, industrial plants, and onto a nice country property with a parklike setting and a creek running along the southern border.

My adult working career began with seven years in retail banking starting as a bookkeeping clerk and working through the various positions to operations officer. I counted many millions of dollars in those years while being paid just a few hundred of them each month. Following that I worked three years in truck leasing starting as rental agent and moving up to district manager. I finally started making a livable wage in 1982 when I went to work for a major oil company as an operator trainee at an oil refinery. In 1989, I left the refinery to work at a cogeneration power plant. I stopped boiling oil and started boiling water instead. I remained in that line of worked until June of 2012 when the effects of an industrial accident that I'd had one year earlier became too much to allow me to continue working.

Two years later it was officially determined that I was no longer fit for duty and too old to be trained on something new.

I'm now "retired" after being gainfully employed since age 12. I'm a college dropout with a refinery process operator certification and a safety specialist certification.

To date, I've written four other books. All four are available on Kindle or in paperback.

"to BE SAFE, YOU should ASSess your safety culture" is a humorous and fairly brief look at several topics to consider when assessing a workplace safety culture. It's written for both blue-collar and white-collar workers. From 1982 to 2012 I worked in industrial plants - oil refining plants and cogeneration power plants. My safety book was written following an on-the-job incident in 2011 that injured me. It also contains the story of that incident and several very funny illustrations created by my oldest son, Justin.

"The Ups and Downs of Love" is a collection of forty-five love poems, originally song lyrics that I wrote beginning in my mid-teens and continuing through to the mid-1990's. The poems are separated into two parts in the book, "The Ups" and "The Downs".

"A Christian Journey" contains the lyrics to over thirty religious songs that I've written. From 1970 to 1982, I often sang at churches on Sundays many times singing my own songs. They were well received back then so I published them as a book of Christian poems.

"Random Thoughts of a Medicated Mind" is a humorous book of thoughts and jokes compiled while I was on medications for PTSD and acute insomnia for a few years following the incident at work in 2011.

Thank you for your interest in this book. I hope you've found it interesting and helpful.

In the event that you got nothing out of it other than a conclusion that the author is filled with nonsense, please let me share one last quote from Galileo:

> *I have never met a man so ignorant that I couldn't learn something from him. — Galileo Galilei*

Best wishes to you in your continuing search for spiritual growth.

Printed in Great Britain
by Amazon